Pocket
VANCOUVER

TOP SIGHTS · LOCAL LIFE · MADE EASY

John Lee

In This Book

QuickStart Guide

Your keys to understanding the city – we help you decide what to do and how to do it

Need to Know
Tips for a smooth trip

Neighborhoods
What's where

Explore Vancouver

The best things to see and do, neighborhood by neighborhood

Top Sights
Make the most of your visit

Local Life
The insider's city

The Best of Vancouver

The city's highlights in handy lists to help you plan

Best Walks
See the city on foot

Vancouver's Best...
The best experiences

Survival Guide

Tips and tricks for a seamless, hassle-free city experience

Getting Around
Travel like a local

Essential Information
Including where to stay

Our selection of the city's best places to eat, drink and experience:

◉ **Sights**

✴ **Eating**

🖳 **Drinking**

✿ **Entertainment**

🔒 **Shopping**

These symbols give you the vital information for each listing:

- ☎ Telephone Numbers
- ⊙ Opening Hours
- P Parking
- ⊖ Nonsmoking
- @ Internet Access
- 🛜 Wi-Fi Access
- 🥗 Vegetarian Selection
- 📖 English-Language Menu
- 👪 Family-Friendly
- 🐾 Pet-Friendly
- 🚌 Bus
- ⛴ Ferry
- Ⓜ Metro
- Ⓢ Subway
- ⊖ London Tube
- 🚊 Tram
- 🚃 Train

Find each listing quickly on maps for each neighborhood:

Bar Hemingway

16 🖳 Map p233, B2

Legend has it that Hemi self, wielding a machine ...rate this timber-pan ...ered bar during ...showpiece is a ...en by Papa ar town. Dress ...s.com; Hôtel Rit ...; ⊙6.30pm-2a

6 ◉ Plac

Lonely Planet's Vancouver

Lonely Planet Pocket Guides are designed to get you straight to the heart of the city.

Inside you'll find all the must-see sights, plus tips to make your visit to each one really memorable. We've split the city into easy-to-navigate neighborhoods and provided clear maps so you'll find your way around with ease. Our expert authors have searched out the best of the city: walks, food, nightlife and shopping, to name a few. Because you want to explore, our 'Local Life' pages will take you to some of the most exciting areas to experience the real Vancouver.

And of course you'll find all the practical tips you need for a smooth trip: itineraries for short visits, how to get around, and how much to tip the guy who serves you a drink at the end of a long day's exploration.

It's your guarantee of a really great experience.

Our Promise

You can trust our travel information because Lonely Planet authors visit the places we write about, each and every edition. We never accept freebies for positive coverage, so you can rely on us to tell it like it is.

QuickStart Guide

Welcome to Vancouver

First-time Vancouver visitors are easy to spot. They're the ones suddenly stopping on the sidewalks after glimpsing the nearby snow-capped peaks framed by downtown's shiny glass towers. But there's more than scenic selfies to Western Canada's biggest city. Walkable neighborhoods, drink-and-dine delights and memorable cultural and outdoor activities make it easy to fall for this lotusland metropolis.

Science World (p72)
KIM ROGERSON/GETTY IMAGES ©

Vancouver
Top Sights

Stanley Park (p24)

Canada's largest urban park offers dramatic forest and mountain-framed seawall vistas plus a 400-hectare woodland studded with trails, attractions and sunset-hugging beaches. Watch for raccoons, beavers and a multitude of chittering bird life.

Museum of Anthropology (p104)

Vancouver's best museum houses one of Canada's finest collections of northwest coast aboriginal art and artifacts. But that's just the start, with countless additional treasures illuminating diverse cultures from around the world.

Granville Island Public Market (p64)

One of Canada's greatest public markets is ideal for an afternoon of perusing deli treats, shiny fruit and vegetable stalls and enticing arts and crafts stands. Market tours recommended.

Capilano Suspension Bridge Park (p118)

A jelly-leg-triggering suspension bridge walk over the tree-flanked waters of Capilano Canyon is a Metro Vancouver must-do. Add the forest trails plus cliff-side and canopy walkways for the full scenery-hugging effect.

VanDusen Botanical Garden (p88)

A delightful alfresco confection of verdant walkways fringed by local and exotic flora: just wandering around the lake here is enough to slow your heart rate to a relaxed level.

Vancouver Art Gallery (p28)

The region's most important gallery, the VAG is a vital part of Vancouver's richly diverse cultural scene. Contemporary exhibitions – often showcasing renowned photoconceptualists – jostle for chin-stroking attention with blockbuster visiting shows.

Vancouver Police Museum (p46)

A hidden gem exposing the seedy underbelly of Vancouver's not-too-distant past. Located in a heritage building that formerly housed a coroner's court and autopsy room. Check your nervous disposition at the entrance.

Dr Sun Yat-Sen Classical Chinese Garden & Park (p48)

This delightful oasis is one of Vancouver's most tranquil ornamental green spaces. Framed by tile-topped walls surrounding a mirror-calm pond, its covered walkways provide sigh-triggering respite from clamorous Chinatown.

Vancouver Local Life

Insider tips to help you find the real city

Vancouver's distinctive districts invite easy on-foot exploring. If you're visiting an attraction, save time to discover the neighborhood it resides in or just plunge right in for a full day or two of local urban adventuring.

West End 'Hood & Heritage Stroll (p30)

▶ Historic homes
▶ Beach vistas

Lined with vintage houses and apartment buildings, this charming residential area is framed by busy thoroughfares Denman, Davie and Robson Sts. Home to Vancouver's thriving gay district, it offers a full menu of dining options plus adjoining Stanley Park for sunset-watching.

Chinatown Culture & History Crawl (p50)

▶ Photogenic heritage
▶ Delightful classical garden

Striped with colorful historic buildings and a sensory explosion of distinctive shops and restaurants, one of Vancouver's most camera-ready neighborhoods has many stories to tell. Take your time while exploring but don't miss the area's unique urban green space.

Off-the-beaten-path Granville Island (p68)

▶ Arts and crafts
▶ Craft booze

There's much more to Granville Island than the Public Market -- just ask the locals. Follow them to the nooks and crannies of this former industrial area for cool shops and studios, shimmering waterfront views and some tasty libation spots.

Commercial Drive Drink & Dine (p82)

▶ Bohemian vibe
▶ Eclectic restaurants

One of Vancouver's most exciting and ever-welcoming streets, the Drive's strollable promenade of unique coffeeshops, ethnically diverse eateries and chain-free boutiques makes this one of the city's great hangout 'hoods. Drop by on a summer evening for top patio action.

Main Street Hipster Stroll (p84)

▶ Indie boutiques
▶ Eclectic dining

Beards and plaid abound in Vancouver's hipster heartland but Main St is also lined with great bars,

University of British Columbia (UBC)

coffeeshops, restaurants and the kind of unique shops that make your credit cards sweat. Expect enticing book, record and fashion emporiums to lure you in.

South Granville Stroll (p90)

▶ Inviting shops
▶ Historic theater

Originally Vancouver's independent gallery district, South Granville is like a bustling high street of boutiques showcasing everything from chocolate to fashions and interior design. Coffee bars and restaurants abound, while one of the city's favorite live theaters also calls this area home.

UBC Campus & Gardens Walk (p106)

▶ Hidden-gem museum
▶ Verdant gardens

Locals have been visiting the attractions at this waterfront university campus for years. But there's much more to discover: off-the-beaten-path lures include hidden artworks, small museums, avant-garde galleries and some breathtaking and beloved green spaces.

Other great places to experience the city like a local:

Catfe (p56)

Paper Hound (p42)

Liberty Distillery (p78)

Storm Crow Alehouse (p97)

Eastside Flea (p60)

Mario's Coffee Express (p38)

Kitsilano Beach (p113)

Bistro 101 (p76)

Pronto (p96)

Vancouver
Day Planner

Day One

Commune with Gassy Jack Deighton's **statue** (p53) in Gastown's **Maple Tree Square**, reflecting on the fact Vancouver might not be here if it wasn't for the pub he built. Too early to tipple? Peruse Water St's cool shops, including **John Fluevog Shoes** (p60).

Chinatown is right next door. Don't miss Pender St's **Chinatown Millennium Gate** (p54) and the aromatic traditional grocery stores on Keefer St. Then divert to the **Vancouver Police Museum** (p46) before ending your afternoon in tranquil **Dr Sun Yat-Sen Classical Chinese Garden** (p51).

Weave back to Gastown's Alexander St and the **Alibi Room** (p56), one of Vancouver's favorite craft-beer bars. Toast your day with a four-flight sampler.

Day Two

Stroll the **Stanley Park** (p24) **seawall**, photograph the **totem poles** and visit the ever-popular **Vancouver Aquarium** (p35). You'll find beady-eyed blue herons at **Lost Lagoon** – duck into the **Stanley Park Nature House** (p34) to learn about them.

Next, wander the adjoining tree-lined West End neighborhood, including Davie and Denman Sts. Save time for **English Bay beach** (p34) and, a few blocks away, **Roedde House Museum** (p34). Coffee and dining spots abound here.

Davie St is the center of Vancouver's gay community, with plenty of nightlife options for folks of all persuasions. Consider a sunset-viewing cocktail at **Sylvia's Lounge** (p39) in the area's ivy-covered heritage hotel.

Short on time?
We've arranged Vancouver's must-sees into these day-by-day itineraries to make sure you see the very best of the city in the time you have available.

Day Three

☀ Climb the hill in **Queen Elizabeth Park** (p94) for breathtaking panoramic city views then duck into nearby **Bloedel Conservatory** (p94), a climate-controlled dome housing tropical flora and bird life.

☀ Depart for nearby **Cambie Village**, a popular parade of shops, bars and restaurants, including pasta-perfect **Pronto** (p96). Store-wise, don't miss **Walrus** (p100) and **Shop Cocoon** (p100).

☾ Next up, **VanDusen Botanical Garden** (p88) is a year-round cornucopia of flowers centered on a large pond loved by turtles, herons and wandering raccoons. Save time to crack the **Elizabethan Maze**.

Day Four

☀ Start at the University of British Columbia's must-see **Museum of Anthropology** (p104) and **Beaty Biodiversity Museum** (p110). Green-thumbed visitors should also add **UBC Botanical Garden** (p110).

☀ Then hop bus 4 to Kitsilano's West 4th Ave for independent shops including **Silk Road Tea** (p116) and **Zulu Records** (p117). Add coffee at **49th Parallel** (p114).

☾ Continue to Granville Island for a **Liberty Distillery** (p65) cocktail before catching a side-splitting **Vancouver Theatresports League** (p79) improv show.

Need to Know

For more information, see Survival Guide (p147)

Currency
Canadian Dollar ($)

Language
English

Visas
Not required for visitors from the US, Commonwealth and most of Western Europe for stays up to 180 days. Required by those from more than 130 other countries. Many visa-exempt foreign nationals flying to Canada require an Electronic Travel Authorization (eTA). See www.canada.ca/eta for information.

Money
ATMs are widely available around the city. Credit cards are widely used at accommodations, shops and restaurants.

Cell Phones
Local SIM cards may be used with some international phones. Roaming can be expensive: check with your service provider.

Time
Pacific Time (GMT/UTC minus eight hours)

Tipping
Tip restaurant wait staff 15%, bar servers $1 per drink, hotel bellhops $1 to $2 per bag, and taxis 10% to 15%.

❶ Before You Go

Your Daily Budget

Budget: Less than $100
- ▶ Dorm bed $35
- ▶ Food-court meal $8
- ▶ Happy-hour beer $5
- ▶ All-day transit pass $9.75

Midrange: $100–$250
- ▶ Double room in standard hotel $150
- ▶ Dinner for two in neighborhood restaurant $40 (excl drinks)
- ▶ Craft beer for two $15
- ▶ Museum entry $15-25

Top End: More than $250
- ▶ Four-star hotel room from $250
- ▶ Fine-dining meal for two $100
- ▶ Cocktails for two $25
- ▶ Taxi trips around Vancouver $5 and up

Useful Websites

Miss 604 (www.miss604.com) Vancouver's favorite blogger.

Tourism Vancouver (www.tourismvancouver. com) Official tourism site.

Lonely Planet (www.lonelyplanet.com/vancouver) Destination information, hotel bookings, traveler forums and more.

Advance Planning

Three months before Book summer hotel stays and popular event tickets.

One month before Book car rentals and top restaurant tables plus theater tickets.

One week before Check www.straight. com listings for imminent events.

② Arriving in Vancouver

✈ From Vancouver International Airport

Situated 13km south of the city in Richmond. Canada Line Skytrain services to downtown typically take around 25 minutes and cost $7.75 to $10.50, depending on the time of day. Alternatively, taxis cost up to $45.

🚍 From Pacific Central Station

Most trains and long-distance buses arrive from across Canada and the US at this station on the southern edge of Chinatown. Across the street is the Main St-Science World SkyTrain station. From there it's just five minutes to downtown ($2.75).

⛴ BC Ferries

Services from Vancouver Island and the Gulf Islands arrive at Tsawwassen, one hour south of Vancouver, or Horseshoe Bay, 30 minutes from downtown in West Vancouver. Both are accessible by regular transit bus services.

③ Getting Around

🚌 Bus

Vancouver's TransLink (www.translink.ca) bus network is extensive. Exact change (or more) is required; buses use fare machines and change is not given. Fares cost adult/child $2.75/1.75 and are valid for up to 90 minutes of transfer travel.

🚌 SkyTrain

TransLink's SkyTrain rapid-transit network is a great way to move around the region, especially beyond the city center.

Tickets for SkyTrain trips can be purchased from station vending machines (change is given; machines also accept debit and credit cards) prior to boarding.

SkyTrain journeys cost $2.75 to $5.50 (plus $5 more if you're traveling from the airport), depending on how far you are journeying and the time of day.

🚌 SeaBus

The SeaBus shuttle is part of the TransLink transit system and it operates throughout the day, taking 12 minutes to cross Burrard Inlet between Waterfront Station and Lonsdale Quay in North Vancouver. At Lonsdale you can connect to buses for North Vancouver and West Vancouver; bus 236 goes to both Capilano Suspension Bridge and Grouse Mountain.

Tickets must be purchased from vending machines on either side of the route before boarding. The machines take credit and debit cards and also give change up to $20 for cash transactions.

🚕 Taxi

Vancouver currently does not allow Uber-type services. Try these taxi companies:

▶ **Black Top & Checker Cabs** (📞604-731-1111)

▶ **Vancouver Taxi** (📞604-871-1111)

▶ **Yellow Cab** (📞604-681-1111)

Vancouver
Neighborhoods

**Downtown &
West End (p22)**
Lined with shops and
restaurants, city center
Vancouver adjoins the
largely residential West
End plus spectacular,
oceanfront Stanley Park.

◉ Top Sights

Stanley Park

Vancouver Art Gallery

◉ *Museum of
Anthropology*

**Kitsilano & University
of British Columbia
(UBC; p102)**
Beaches and heritage
homes lure the locals to
Kits while the nearby
campus has some top
day-out attractions.

◉ Top Sight

Museum of
Anthropology

Worth a Trip

◯ Local Life

Commercial Drive (p82)

Main Street (p84)

Worth a Trip

👁 **Top Sight**

Capilano Suspension Bridge Park (p118)

Gastown & Chinatown (p44)

Side-by-side historic neighborhoods studded with some of Vancouver's best bars, restaurants and one-of-a-kind boutiques.

👁 **Top Sights**

Vancouver Police Museum

Dr Sun Yat-Sen Classical Chinese Garden & Park

Yaletown & Granville Island (p62)

On opposite sides of False Creek, these enticing areas host some of the city's best shopping and dining options.

👁 **Top Sight**

Granville Island Public Market

Fairview & South Granville (p86)

Twin residential areas with highly walkable shopping and dining streets plus some great green attractions.

👁 **Top Sight**

VanDusen Botanical Garden

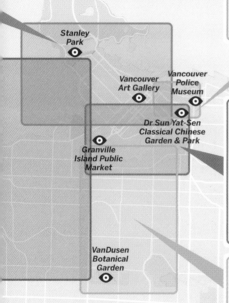

Stanley Park 👁

Vancouver Art Gallery 👁

Vancouver Police Museum 👁

Dr Sun Yat-Sen Classical Chinese Garden & Park 👁

Granville Island Public Market 👁

VanDusen Botanical Garden 👁

Explore
Vancouver

Worth a Trip

Vancouver harbor and city skyline
DAN BRECKWOLDT/SHUTTERSTOCK ©

Explore

Downtown & West End

The heart of Vancouver occupies an ocean-fringed peninsula easily divided into three: the grid-pattern city center of shops, restaurants and businesses radiating from the intersection of Granville and West Georgia Sts; the 1950s towers and dense residential side streets of the West End (also home to Vancouver's gay district); and Canada's greatest urban green space, spectacular Stanley Park.

The Sights in a Day

☀ Catch some early morning rays on a seawall **Stanley Park** (p24) walk, saving time for beachside photos and an introduction to the region's flora and fauna at the **Stanley Park Nature House** (p34). A morning visit to the **Vancouver Aquarium** (p35) is also recommended for sidestepping the summer crowds at this popular attraction.

☀ Depart the park and stroll the manicured residential side streets of the West End, stopping for lunch at Robson's St's **Forage** (p36). There are also plenty of shopping and coffee pit stops to consider on Denman and Davie Sts. Once you've snagged all your souvenirs, hunt down some of the historic, brightly painted wooden heritage houses that still line this area.

☾ Point yourself towards the center of downtown along Robson St, perusing the boutiques lining this popular shopping strip. Then head to the waterfront and the pier-like promenade at **Canada Place** (p34). It's ideal for catching a sunset view of the North Shore mountains. Dinnertime? The lip-smacking **Royal Dinette** (p36) is just a short stroll away.

For a local's day in the West End, see p30.

◉ **Top Sights**

Stanley Park (p24)

Vancouver Art Gallery (p28)

🔍 **Local Life**

West End 'Hood & Heritage Stroll (p30)

💜 **Best of Vancouver**

Eating

Forage (p36)

Jam Cafe (p36)

Entertainment

Commodore Ballroom (p40)

Theatre Under the Stars (p41)

Shopping

Paper Hound (p42)

Getting There

🚃 **Train** SkyTrain trundles through downtown.

🚌 **Bus** The number 5 runs along Robson St, 6 along Davie, 10 along Granville and 19 into Stanley Park.

🚗 **Car** There are car parks and parking meters throughout the area.

Top Sights
Stanley Park

One of North America's largest urban green spaces, Stanley Park is revered for its dramatic forest-and-mountain oceanfront views. But there's more to this 400-hectare woodland than looks. The park is studded with nature-hugging trails, family-friendly attractions, sunset-loving beaches and tasty places to eat. There's also the occasional unexpected sight to search for (besides the raccoons that call the place home).

👁 Map p32, D1

🅿 🚻

🚌 19

Stanley Park seawall

Seawall

Built in stages between 1917 and 1980, the park's 8.8km **seawall** trail is Vancouver's favorite outdoor hangout. Encircling the park, it offers spectacular waterfront vistas on one side and dense forest on the other. You can walk the whole thing in roughly three hours or rent a bike to cover the route faster. Keep in mind: cyclists and rollerbladers must travel counterclockwise on the seawall, so there's no going back once you start your trundle.

About 1.5km from the W Georgia St entrance, you'll come to the ever-popular totem poles. Remnants of an abandoned 1930s plan to create a First Nations 'theme village,' the bright-painted poles were joined by the addition of three exquisitely carved Coast Salish welcome arches a few years back. For the full First Nations story, consider a fascinating guided park walk with Talaysay Tours.

Natural Attractions

You don't have to be a child to enjoy Stanley Park's signature attraction. The Vancouver Aquarium (p35) combines exotic marine species with re-created local seascapes. Also check out the mesmerizing iridescent jellyfish, and peruse the schedule for feeding times: there's almost always one hungry animal or another waiting for its dinner.

The aquarium isn't Stanley Park's only hot spot for flora and fauna fans. A few steps from the park's W Georgia St entrance lies **Lost Lagoon**, which was originally part of Coal Harbour. A bird-beloved nature sanctuary – keep your eyes peeled for blue herons – its perimeter pathway is a favored stroll for wildlife nuts. The Stanley Park Nature House (p34) here has exhibits on the

☑ **Top Tips**

▶ It typically takes around three hours to walk the 8.8km Stanley Park seawall, but bike rentals are also available on nearby Denman St.

▶ In summer, the seawall is packed with visitors; arrive early morning or early evening if tranquil nature-communing is your bag.

▶ There are often summertime queues to enter the Vancouver Aquarium; make it one of your first stops when you arrive at the park.

✗ **Take a Break**

▶ The park's Stanley's Bar & Grill (p38) is a fun spot for a patio beer among the trees.

▶ There is a cornucopia of great Asian eateries near the park on Denman and Robson Sts; consider Sura Korean Cuisine (p37).

park's wildlife, history and ecology – ask about their well-priced guided walks.

Beaches & Views

If it's sandy beaches you're after, the park has several alluring options. **Second Beach** is a family-friendly area on the park's western side, with a grassy playground, an ice-cream-serving concession and a huge outdoor swimming **pool.** For a little more tranquility, try **Third Beach.** A sandy expanse with plenty of logs to sit against, this is a favored summer-evening destination for Vancouverites. The sky often comes alive with pyrotechnic color, while chilled out locals munch through their picnics.

There's a plethora of additional vistas in the park, but perhaps the most popular is at **Prospect Point.** One of Vancouver's best lookouts, this lofty spot is located at the park's northern tip. In summer, you'll be jostling for elbow room with tour parties; heading down the steep stairs to the viewing platform usually shakes them off. Also look out for scavenging raccoons here (don't pet them).

Statue Spotting

Stanley Park is studded with statues, all of which come to life at night (OK, just kidding). On your leisurely amble around the tree-lined idyll, look out for the following and award yourself 10 points for each one you find. If you're on the seawall, it shouldn't be

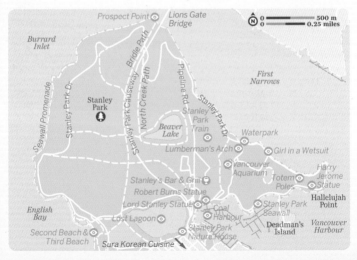

hard to spot *Girl in a Wetsuit*, a 1972 bronze by Elek Imredy that sits in the water. But how about the Robbie Burns statue unveiled by British Prime Minister Ramsay MacDonald in 1928 or the dramatic bronze of Canadian sprint legend Harry Jerome, who held six world records and won a bronze at the 1964 Summer Olympics?

For Kids

It's doesn't take much to plan an entire day with children here. As well as the aquarium and the Nature House, there are a couple of additional must-dos for under-10s. Look out for the large **waterpark** overlooking the waterfront near Lumberman's Arch. There's also a playground here.

Dry the kids off with a ride on the **Stanley Park Train**; just a short stroll from the aquarium, this popular replica of the first passenger train that rolled into Vancouver in 1887 is a firm family favorite. The ride assumes several additional incarnations during the year: at Halloween it's dressed up for ghost fans; and from late November it becomes a Christmas-decorated theme ride that's the city's most popular family-friendly Yuletide activity.

If it's still light when you're leaving the park, visit the man behind the fun

Girl in a Wetsuit statue by Elek Imredy

day you've just had. Take the ramp running parallel with the seawall near the W Georgia St entrance and you'll find an almost-hidden **statue of Lord Stanley** with his arms outstretched, nestled in the trees. On his plinth are the words he used at the park's 1889 dedication ceremony: 'To the use and enjoyment of people of all colors, creeds and customs for all time.' It's a sentiment that still resonates loudly here today.

Top Sights
Vancouver Art Gallery

Colonizing a heritage courthouse building, but aiming for a fancy new venue in the coming years, the VAG is the region's most important art gallery. Transforming itself in recent decades, it's also a vital part of the city's cultural scene. Contemporary exhibitions – sometimes showcasing the Vancouver School of photoconceptualists – are combined with blockbuster traveling shows from around the world.

⊙ Map p32, G4

☏ 604-662-4700

www.vanartgallery.bc.ca

750 Hornby St

adult/child $20/6

🕙 10am-5pm Wed-Mon, to 9pm Tue

🚍 5

VAG 101

Before you arrive at the VAG, check online for details of the latest exhibition: the biggest shows of the year here are typically in summer, and it's often a good idea to arrive early or late in the day to avoid the crush, especially at the beginning or end of an exhibition's run. But the VAG isn't just about blockbusters. If you have time, explore this landmark gallery's other offerings. Start on the top floor, where British Columbia's most famous painter is often showcased. Emily Carr (1871–1945) is celebrated for her swirling, nature-inspired paintings of regional landscapes and First Nations culture. Watercolors were her main medium, and the gallery has a large collection of her works.

Join the Locals

The gallery isn't just a place to geek out over cool art. In fact, locals treat it as an important part of their social calendar. Every few months, the VAG stages its regular **FUSE** socials, which transform the domed heritage venue into a highly popular evening event with DJs, bars, live performances and quirky gallery tours. Vancouverites dress up and treat the event as one of the highlights of the city's art scene; expect a clubby vibe to pervade proceedings.

New Gallery

The VAG has been complaining about the limitations of its heritage-building venue for many years and plans have recently been announced for a new and far larger purpose-built art museum a few blocks away on W Georgia St. At time of research, the architect-designed plans resembled a dramatic array of wooden blocks piled on top of each other. Check the VAG's website for updates.

☑ Top Tips

▶ If you're visiting in winter, you'll find the VAG's standard ticket prices reduced by a few dollars.

▶ You can save on admission any time of the year on Tuesday evenings between 5pm and 9pm, when entry is by-donation.

▶ Seniors can also partake of by donation entry on the first Monday of every month between 10am and 1pm.

▶ Check the VAG's online calendar for in-depth curator tours; these are free with admission.

✕ Take a Break

▶ The large patio of the onsite Gallery Cafe (p37) is a great spot to grab a coffee and people-watch over bustling Robson St.

▶ For a fancy dinner to conclude your artsy day out, chic Hawksworth (p37) is just a few steps away.

Local Life
West End 'Hood & Heritage Stroll

One of Vancouver's most attractive residential areas, the West End combines clapboard houses with art deco apartment buildings. Home of the city's bustling gay district (look out for the rainbow-hued crosswalk), there's also a full menu of places to join the locals for coffee, drinks or dinner, especially on the main Denman St and Davie St thoroughfares.

1 Stroll Denman Street
You'll pass alongside dozens of mid-priced, mostly non-chain restaurants on lively Denman, ranging from Japanese *izakayas* to Spanish tapas joints; choose one to return to later for dinner. There are also plenty of enticing shops to attract your wallet as you wander in the direction of the waterfront.

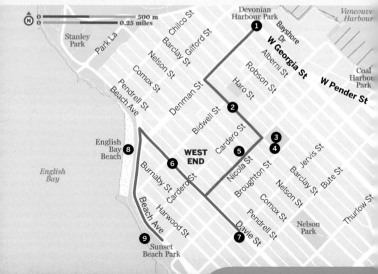

2 Check out Barclay Street's Historic Homes

This street is the residential heart of Vancouver's gay community. There are some smashing 1950s and older heritage apartment buildings plus plenty of beautifully maintained wooden Arts and Crafts homes, often painted in bright colors.

3 Peruse Barclay Heritage Square's Antique Houses

A well-preserved plaza of late Victorian houses, the square is a reminder of how the well-to-do Vancouverites of yesteryear lived. Look out for dainty stained-glass windows and wide clapboard verandahs here.

4 Visit Roedde House Museum

For a glimpse behind the lace curtains, drop into this lovely, antique-lined **house museum** (p34). You'll find rooms – from kitchen to parlor to bedrooms – teeming with period details, as if the residents have just stepped out.

5 Pass Alongside Firehall No 6

Nicola St is also lined with older buildings, including this 1907-built redbrick firehall. It's still in use but has the feel (and look) of a heritage-hugging museum. There's often a shiny fire truck basking in the sun outside.

6 Mooch Down Davie Street

Arguably even busier than Denman, Davie is flanked with shops and cafes. This is also the main commercial hub for the city's gay community; keep your eyes peeled for the pink-painted bus shelters. There are plenty of bars and clubs here.

7 Coffee at Melriches

Sip on a large hot chocolate at this cosy **coffeehouse** (p40). Grab a window seat to watch the busy Davie St action outside.

8 Vista-watching at English Bay Beach

Snap a few photos of the delightful *A-maze-ing Laughter* public artwork of 14 chuckling bronze figures then hit the beach, one of the most popular summertime hangouts in the city. You'll find wonderful panoramic ocean views here.

9 Grassy Rest Stop at Sunset Beach

Sit on a grassy bank, soak up the rays and watch the fit Vancouverites jog and rollerblade by. Alternatively, catch a miniferry from here to Granville Island, which is winking at you just across the water.

A B C D

1

N

0 — 500 m
0 — 0.25 miles

Bridle Path

Stanley Park Causeway

Stanley Park

Stanley Park Dr

Lost Lagoon Dr

Lost Lagoon

Stanley Park Nature House 1

2

Seawall Promenade

Stanley Park Pitch & Putt

Lagoon Dr

Park La

Chilco St

Gilford St

Denman St

3

Beach Ave

20

24

Bidwell St

English Bay Beach 4

Beach Ave

WEST EN

Davie St

English Bay

Nicola St

4

Broughton S

Sunset Beach Park

False Creek

5

For reviews see

Top Sights	p24
Sights	p34
Eating	p36
Drinking	p38
Entertainment	p40
Shopping	p42

Hadden Park

Vanier Park

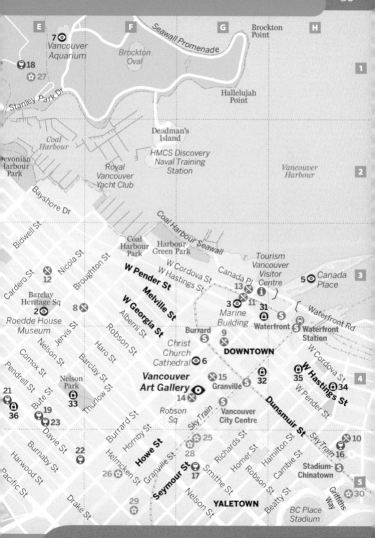

E 7 Vancouver Aquarium

18

27

F Brockton Oval

Seawall Promenade

G Brockton Point

H

1

Stanley Park Dr

Coal Harbour

evonian
Harbour
Park

Bayshore Dr

Bidwell St

Deadman's
Island

HMCS Discovery
Naval Training
Station

Royal
Vancouver
Yacht Club

Vancouver
Harbour

2

Coal Harbour Seawall

Nicola St

Cardero St

12

Barclay
Heritage Sq

2

Roedde House
Museum

Comox St

Pendrell St

21

36

Broughton St

8

Jervis St

Nelson St

Bute St

19

23

Burnaby St

Nelson
Park

33

Barclay St

Haro St

Robson St

Alberni St

W Pender St

Melville St

W Georgia St

Burrard

Christ
Church
Cathedral

6

Vancouver
Art Gallery

14

Robson
Sq

Coal
Harbour
Park

Harbour
Green Park

W Cordova St
W Hastings St

Canada Pl

13

3

Marine
Building

9

Tourism
Vancouver
Visitor
Centre

11

31

Waterfront

5

Canada
Place

3

Waterfront Rd

Waterfront
Station

W Cordova St

DOWNTOWN

15

Granville

32

35

W Hastings St

34

4

Dunsmuir St

W Pender St

SkyTrain

2

Pacific St

Drake St

Harwood St

22

26

Davie St

Thurlow St

Burrard St

Hornby St

Howe St

Helmcken St

Granville St

Seymour St

25

28

17

29

Smithe St

Richards St

Homer St

Robson St

Vancouver
City Centre

SkyTrain

Nelson St

Hamilton St

Cambie St

YALETOWN

Beatty St

Stadium-
Chinatown

10

16

30

5

Griffiths
Way

BC Place
Stadium

Sights

Stanley Park Nature House
NATURE RESERVE

1 ◎ Map p32, D2

Illuminating the breathtaking array of flora and fauna just steps from the busy streets of the West End, this charming nature center is a great introduction to the wild side of Stanley Park. The chatty volunteers will tell you all you need to know about the area's critters, from coyotes to Douglas squirrels and from blue herons to black-capped chickadees. Book ahead for guided nature walks or just wander the park's trails on your own, armed with your new-found wildlife expertise. (☑604-257-8544; www. stanleyparkecology.ca; north end of Alberni St, Lost Lagoon; admission free; ◷10am-5pm Tue-Sun Jul & Aug, 10am-4pm Sat & Sun Sep-Jun; 👶; 🚌19)

Roedde House Museum
MUSEUM

2 ◎ Map p32, E3

For a glimpse of what the West End looked like before the apartment blocks arrived, drop by this handsome 1893 Queen Anne–style mansion, now a lovingly preserved museum. Designed by infamous British Columbia (BC) architect Francis Rattenbury, the house is packed with antiques and the garden is planted in period style. Admission comes with a guided tour, while Sunday entry includes tour, tea and cookies for just $8. (☑604-684-

7040; www.roeddehouse.org; 1415 Barclay St; $5; ◷11am-4pm Tue-Sat, 1-4pm Sun, reduced hours in winter; 🚌5)

Marine Building
HISTORIC BUILDING

3 ◎ Map p32, G3

Vancouver's most romantic old-school tower block, and also its best art deco building, the elegant 22-story Marine Building is a tribute to the city's maritime past. Check out the elaborate exterior of seahorses, lobsters and streamlined ships, then nip into the lobby where it's like a walk-through artwork. Stained-glass panels and a polished floor inlaid with signs of the zodiac await. (355 Burrard St; Ⓢ Burrard)

English Bay Beach
BEACH

4 ◎ Map p32, C3

Wandering south on Denman St, you'll spot a clutch of palm trees ahead announcing one of Canada's best urban beaches. Then you'll see Vancouver's most popular public artwork: a series of oversized laughing figures that makes everyone smile. There's a party atmosphere here in summer as locals catch rays and panoramic ocean views...or just ogle the volleyballers prancing around on the sand. (cnr Denman St & Beach Ave; 🚌5)

Canada Place
LANDMARK

5 ◎ Map p32, H3

Vancouver's version of the Sydney Opera House – judging by the number of postcards it appears on – this iconic

MICHAEL WHEATLEY/AGEFOTOSTOCK ©

Marine Building

landmark is shaped like sails jutting into the sky over the harbor. Both a cruise-ship terminal and convention center (next door's grass-roofed expansion opened in 2010), it's also a stroll-worthy pier, providing photogenic views of the North Shore mountains and some busy floatplane action. (☎604-775-7063; www.canadaplace.ca; 999 Canada Place Way; P; S Waterfront)

Christ Church Cathedral
CATHEDRAL

6 ◎ Map p32, G4

Completed in 1895 and designated as a cathedral in 1929, the city's most attractive gothic-style church is nestled incongruously alongside looming

glass towers. It's home to a wide range of cultural events, including regular choir and chamber music recitals and the occasional Shakespeare reading. The roof was being replaced and a new stained-glass-accented bell tower was being added on our visit. (☎604-682-3848; www.thecathedral.ca; 690 Burrard St; ⊙10am-4pm; S Burrard)

Vancouver Aquarium
AQUARIUM

7 ◎ Map p32, E1

Stanley Park's biggest draw, the aquarium is home to 9000 water-loving critters – including sharks, wolf eels and a somewhat shy octopus. There's also a small, walk-through rainforest area of birds, turtles and a statue-still sloth. The aquarium also keeps captive whales and dolphins and organizes animal encounters with these creatures, which may concern some visitors. Animal-welfare groups claim keeping cetaceans in enclosed tanks is harmful for these complex animals. (☑604-659-3400; www.vanaqua.org; 845 Avison Way; adult/child $31/22; ☉9:30am-6pm Jul & Aug, 10am-5pm Sep-Jun; ; ☐19)

Eating

Forage

CANADIAN $$

8 Map p32, E3

A champion of the local farm-to-table scene, this sustainability-friendly restaurant is the perfect way to sample the flavors of the region. Brunch has become a firm local favorite (turkey-sausage hash recommended), and for dinner the idea is to sample an array of tasting plates. The menu is innovative and highly seasonal, but look out for the seafood chowder with quail's egg. Reservations recommended. (☑604-661-1400; www.foragevancouver.com; 1300 Robson St; mains $16-29; ☉6:30-10am & 5pm-midnight Mon-Fri, 7am-2pm & 5pm-midnight Sat & Sun; ☐5)

Royal Dinette

INTERNATIONAL $$

9 Map p32, G4

Seasonal and regional are the foundations of this smashing downtown restaurant, but add friendly, unpretentious service and it becomes a winner. The lunchtime two- or three-course

prix fixe ($30 or $35) is a good way to try the place out, but dinner is all about a lingering opportunity to savor international influences combined with local ingredients: the squid-ink spaghetti is our favorite. (☑604-974-8077; www.royaldinette.ca; 905 Dunsmuir St; mains $15-34; ☉11:30am-2pm & 5-10pm; Ⓢ Burrard)

Jam Cafe

BREAKFAST $$

10 Map p32, H5

The Vancouver outpost of Victoria's wildly popular breakfast and brunch superstar hit the ground running soon after opening here. It's typically packed: you will have to wait for a table (reservations are not accepted) unless you're smart enough to dine very off-peak. You will find a white-walled room that is studded with Canadian knickknacks and a huge array of satisfying options, from chicken and waffles to red-velvet pancakes. (☑778-379-1992; www.jamcafes.com; 556 Beatty St; mains $11-16; ☉8am-3pm; ; Ⓢ Stadium-Chinatown)

Tractor

CANADIAN $

11 Map p32, G3

A healthy fast-food cafeteria that is tucked into the base of the Marine Building. Step up to the counter and choose from 10 or so hearty mixed salads, then add a half or whole grilled sandwich. Wholesome and satisfying housemade soups and stews are also available but make sure you add a lemonade as well – there's usually a tempting flavor or

two. (📞604-979-0550; www.tractorfoods.
com; Marine Building, 335 Burrard St;
🕙7am-9:30pm Mon-Fri, 11am-9:30pm Sat &
Sun; 🍴; Ⓢ Waterfront)

Sura Korean Cuisine   KOREAN $$

12 Map p32, E3

From the 1400-block of Robson St
on and around onto Denman and
Davie Sts, you'll find a smorgasbord
of authentic Korean and Japanese
eateries. A cut above its ESL-student-
luring siblings, slick Sura offers
awesome Korean comfort dishes in a
cosy, bistrolike setting. Try the spicy
beef soup, kimchi pancakes and excellent *bibimbap*: beef, veggies and a
still-cooking egg in a hot stone bowl.
(📞604-687-7872; www.surakoreancuisine.
com; 1518 Robson St; mains $10-20; 🕙11am-
4pm & 5-10:30pm; 🅿; 🚇5)

Bella Gelateria   ICE CREAM $

13 Map p32, G3

A sunny-day pilgrimage spot that's
often jam-packed with locals trying to
eat their body weight in gelato. There
are classics, like chocolate, but ask for
a sample or two of something more
exotic; the sure fire way to discover if
you'll fall for lavender and Earl Grey
or *akbar mashti* (saffron) is to snag a
free taste (and then another). (📞604-
569-1010; www.bellagelateria.com; 1001 W
Cordova St; 🕙11am-10pm Sun-Thu, to 11pm
Fri & Sat; Ⓢ Waterfront)

Gallery Café   CAFE $

14 Map p32, G4

The Vancouver Art Gallery's
mezzanine-level cafe is a chatty indoor
dining area complemented by possibly
downtown's best and biggest patio.
The food is generally of the salad-and-
sandwiches variety, but it's well worth
stopping in for a drink, especially if
you take your coffee (or bottled beer)
out to the parasol-forested outdoor
area to watch the Robson St action.
(📞604-688-2233; www.thegallerycafe.ca;
750 Hornby St; mains $5-12; 🕙9am-9pm
Mon-Fri, 9:30am-6pm Sat & Sun, reduced
hours off-season; 🚇5)

Hawksworth   WEST COAST $$$

15 Map p32, G4

This chic, fine-dining anchor of the
top-end Rosewood Hotel Georgia is a
popular see-and-be-seen spot. Created

⭕ Local Life
Perfect Picnic

Vancouver is striped with delightful
green spaces that invite alfresco
dining. But it's easy to forget your
picnic hamper when you're pack-
ing for a trip to the city. Luckily,
Picnix Al Fresco To Go (Map p32, D3;
📞778-889-7706; www.picnix.ca; 1725
Davie St; meal $25-40; 🕙noon-3pm &
6-9pm; 🚇5) can supply all the gear
you need for a great outdoor meal
in Stanley Park, including cleverly
designed baskets, blankets and
gourmet food and drinks.

by and named after one of the city's top local chefs, its menu fuses contemporary West Coast approaches with clever international influences, hence dishes such as soy-roasted sturgeon. The seasonal tasting menu is also heartily recommended. (☏ 604-673-7000; www.hawksworthrestaurant.com; 801 W Georgia St; mains $42-55; ⏱ 6:30am-11pm; P; S Vancouver City Centre)

Drinking

Devil's Elbow Ale & Smoke House

PUB

16  Map p32, H5

A cavelike brick-and-art-lined pub that feels like a local secret, this is the place to combine barbecued grub with brews from one of BC's best microbreweries. It is owned by the team that is behind Squamish's Howe Sound Brewing. You'll find great ales to try, from Hopraiser IPA to Father John's Winter Ale. The weekday $15 beer-included lunch deal is recommended. (☏ 604-559-0611; www.devilselbowalehouse.com; 562 Beatty St; ⏱ 11:30am-midnight Mon-Thu, 11:30am-1am Fri, 10am-1am Sat, 10am-midnight Sun; S Stadium-Chinatown)

Uva Wine & Cocktail Bar

LOUNGE

17 Map p32, G5

This sexy nook fuses a heritage mosaic floor with a dash of mod class. But, despite the cool appearances, there's a snob-free approach that encourages taste-tripping through an extensive by-the-glass wine menu and some dangerously delicious cocktails – we love the Spellbound. Food is part of the mix (including shareable small plates) and the daily 2pm to 6pm happy hour is ideal for extended discount quaffing. (☏ 604-632-9560; www.uvavancouver.com; 900 Seymour St; ⏱ 11:30am-2pm; ♙10)

Stanley's Bar & Grill

BAR

18 Map p32, E1

Tucked into one end of the handsome, century-old Stanley Park Pavilion. Snag a patio seat under the gigantic red parasols and grab a beery respite from your exhausting day of park exploring. There's a full range of Stanley Park Brewing tipples (not actually

WILLIAM MANNING/ALAMY STOCK PHOTO ©

Stanley's Bar & Grill

made in the park) plus some good pub grub; the barbecued salmon sandwich is especially recommended. (☏604-602-3088; www.stanleyparkpavilion.com; 610 Pipeline Rd; ◷9am-8pm Jul & Aug, 9am-5pm Sep-Jun; ☐19)

1181   GAY

19 🚇 Map p32, E4

A popular gay bar for those who like posing (or just looking), this loungy spot combines a sofa-strewn front space with a cozy back area that feels more intimate. Separating the two is a side bar staffed by cooler-than-you servers: this is also where the singletons sit, so you can expect to be the subject of some flirty attention if

you prop yourself here. (☏604-787-7130; www.1181.ca; 1181 Davie St; ◷6pm-3am; ☐6)

Sylvia's Lounge   BAR

20 🚇 Map p32, D3

Part of the permanently popular Sylvia Hotel, this was Vancouver's first cocktail bar when it opened in the mid-1950s. Now a comfy, wood-lined neighborhood bar favored by in-the-know locals (they're the ones hogging the window seats as the sun sets dramatically over English Bay), it's a great spot for an end-of-day wind down. There's live music here on Wednesdays and Thursdays. (☏604-681-9321; www.sylviahotel.com; 1154 Gilford St; ◷7am-11pm Sun-Thu, to midnight Fri & Sat; ☐5)

Melriches Coffeehouse   COFFEE

21 🚇 Map p32, E4

With its mismatched wooden tables, an array of hearty cakes and crowd of journal-writing locals hunkered in every corner, this is an ideal rainy-day nook. Warm your hands on a pail-sized hot chocolate and press your face to the window to watch the Davie St locals bustling past. If you're hungry, the cookies are of the giant-sized variety here. (📞604-689-5282; 1244 Davie St; ⏰6am-9:30pm Mon-Sat, 7am-10pm Sun; 🛜; 🚇6)

Fountainhead Pub   GAY

22 🚇 Map p32, E5

The area's loudest and proudest gay neighborhood pub, this friendly joint is all about the patio, which spills onto Davie St like an over-turned wine glass. Take part in the ongoing summer-evening pastime of ogling passing locals or retreat to a quieter spot inside for a few lagers or a naughty cocktail: anyone for a Porn Star or a Red Stag Sour? (📞604-687-2222; www.thefountainheadpub.com; 1025 Davie St; ⏰11am-1am Sun-Thu, to 2am Fri & Sat; 🚇6)

Pumpjack Pub   GAY

23 🚇 Map p32, E4

Glancing through the open window as you walk past on a summer night tells you all you need to know about this popular gay pub: it's a great place to meet leather-clad, often hairy locals ever-ready to make a new friend in town for a quick visit. Expect queues here on weekends as the local bears vie for a pick up or two. (www.pumpjack pub.com; 1167 Davie St; ⏰1pm-2am; 🚇6)

Delany's Coffee House   COFFEE

24 🚇 Map p32, D3

A laid-back, wood-lined neighborhood coffee bar that's the java-hugging heart of the West End's gay community, Delany's is a good perch from which to catch the annual Pride Parade, although you'll have to get here early if you want a front-row seat. The usual array of cookies and muffins will keep you fortified while you wait.

A good spot to pick up a take-out coffee for a stroll to nearby English Bay beach. (📞604-662-3344; www.delanyscoffeehouse.com; 1105 Denman St; ⏰6am-8pm Mon-Fri, 6:30am-8:30pm Sat & Sun; 🛜; 🚇5)

Entertainment

Commodore Ballroom   LIVE MUSIC

25 ⭐ Map p32, G5

Local bands know they've made it when they play Vancouver's best mid-sized venue, a restored art-deco ballroom that still has the city's bounciest dance floor – courtesy of tires placed under its floorboards. If you need a break from your moshing, collapse at one of the tables lining the perimeter, catch your breath with a bottled Stella and then plunge back in. (📞604-739-4550; www.commodoreballroom.com; 868 Granville St; 🚇10)

Orpheum Theatre (p42)

Pacific Cinémathèque   CINEMA

26 ⭐ Map p32, F5

This beloved cinema operates like an ongoing film festival with a daily-changing program of movies. A $3 annual membership is required – organize it at the door – before you can skulk in the dark with other chin-stroking movie buffs who probably named their children (or pets) after Fellini and Bergman. (📞 604-688-3456; www.thecinematheque.ca; 1131 Howe St; tickets $11, double bills $16; 🚍10)

Theatre Under the Stars   PERFORMING ARTS

27 ⭐ Map p32, E1

The old-school Malkin Bowl is an atmospheric open-air venue for summertime shows. The season never gets too serious, usually featuring two enthusiastically performed Broadway musicals, but it's hard to beat the location, especially as the sun fades over the trees peeking from behind the stage. (📞877-840-0457, 604-734-1917; www.tuts.ca; Malkin Bowl, Stanley Park, 610 Pipeline Rd; tickets from $29; 🕐 Jul & Aug; 🚍19)

Orpheum Theatre

THEATER

28 Map p32, G5

Opened in 1927, Vancouver's grandest old-school theater venue has a gorgeous and beautifully maintained baroque interior, making it the perfect place to catch a rousing show with the Vancouver Symphony Orchestra, who calls this place home. There are frequent additional performers here throughout the year; check ahead to see what's on during your stay. The theater is also a National Historic Site. (☎604-665-3050; 601 Smithe St; 🚍10)

Vancity Theatre

CINEMA

29 Map p32, F5

The state-of-the-art headquarters of the **Vancouver International Film Festival** (www.viff.org; ☾late Sep) screens a wide array of movies throughout the year in the kind of auditorium that

Local Life

Bookworms' favorite

Proving that the printed word is alive and kicking, downtown's **Paper Hound** (Map p32, H4; ☎604-428-1344; www.paperhound.ca; 344 W Pender St; ☾10am-7pm Sun-Thu, to 8pm Fri & Sat; 🚍14) bookstore is a small but perfectly curated shop. You'll find tempting texts (mostly used but some new) on everything from nature to poetry to chaos theory. Ask for staff recommendations; they really know their stuff.

cinephiles dream of: generous legroom, wide armrests and great sight lines from each of its 175 seats. (☎604-683-3456; www.viff.org/theatre; 1181 Seymour St; tickets $12, double bills $18; 🚍10)

Vancouver Canucks

HOCKEY

30 Map p32, H5

Vancouver's National Hockey League (NHL) team toyed with fans in 2011's Stanley Cup finals before losing Game 7 to the Boston Bruins, triggering riots across the city. But love runs deep and 'go Canucks, go!' is still boomed out from a packed Rogers Arena at most games. Book your seat early or just head to a local bar for some raucous game-night atmosphere. (☎604-899-7400; http://canucks.nhl.com; Rogers Arena, 800 Griffiths Way; §Stadium-Chinatown)

Shopping

Mink Chocolates

FOOD

31 Map p32, G3

If chocolate is the main food group in your book, follow your candy-primed nose to this designer choccy shop in the downtown core. Select a handful of souvenir bonbons – little edible artworks embossed with prints of trees and coffee cups – then hit the drinks bar for the best velvety hot choc you've ever tasted. Then have another. (☎604-633-2451; www.minkchocolates.com; 863 W Hastings St; ☾7:30am-6pm Mon-Fri, 10am-6pm Sat & Sun; 🛜; §Waterfront)

Golden Age Collectables · BOOKS

32 🔒 Map p32, G4

If you're missing your regular dose of *Emily the Strange* or you just want to blow your vacation budget on a highly detailed life-sized model of Ultra Man, head straight to this Aladdin's cave of the comic-book world. While the clientele is unsurprisingly dominated by males, the staff is friendly and welcoming – especially to wide-eyed kids buying their first *Archie*. (📞604-683-2819; www.gacvan.com; 852 Granville St; ⏰10am-9pm Mon-Sat, 11am-6pm Sun; 🚇10)

West End Farmers Market · MARKET

33 🔒 Map p32, E4

Vancouver's most urban alfresco farmers market is in the heart of the West End. It runs during the sunniest months of the year (but doesn't stop for rain), and it's a great way to meet the locals. The strip of 30 or so stalls often includes baked treats, arts and crafts, and glistening piles of freshly picked, locally grown fruit and veg. (📞604-879-3276; www.eatlocal.org; Comox St, btwn Bute & Thurlow Sts, Nelson Park; ⏰9am-2pm Sat Jun–mid-Oct; 🚇6)

Vinyl Records · MUSIC

34 🔒 Map p32, H4

Recently relocated and now one of Vancouver's largest used (mostly) record shops. You'll need hours to sort through the higgledy-piggledy array of crates and cardboard boxes housing everything from polka to Pink Floyd. Make sure you know your prices since not everything is a bargain – most of the sale items are gathered near the front of the shop. (📞604-488-1234; www.vinylrecords.ca; 319 W Hastings St; ⏰noon-6pm Mon-Sat, 1-5pm Sun; 🚇14)

Vancouver Pen Shop · FASHION & ACCESSORIES

35 🔒 Map p32, H4

There are two things about this store that are pleasingly old-fashioned: the staff greet you when you walk in and ask how to help you, and the items they're selling harken to a bygone age when fine pens and penmanship were important markers (no pun intended) of civilization. It's not all gold-nibbed fountain pens, though: there are writing tools for every budget here. (📞604-681-1612; 512 W Hastings St; ⏰9:30am-5:30pm Mon-Fri, 10am-5pm Sat; 🄂Waterfront)

Little Sister's Book & Art Emporium · BOOKS, ACCESSORIES

36 🔒 Map p32, E4

One of the few gay bookshops in western Canada, Little Sister's is a large bazaar of queer-positive tomes, plus magazines, DVDs and toys of the adult type. If this is your first visit to Vancouver, it's a great place to network with the local 'gayborhood.' Check the noticeboards for events and announcements from the wider community. (📞604-669-1753; www.littlesisters.ca; 1238 Davie St; ⏰9am-11pm; 🚇6)

Explore

Gastown & Chinatown

The gentrifying heritage buildings of Vancouver's cobbled old-town district, Gastown now houses some of the city's best independent shops, bars and restaurants. Almost as old, Vancouver's Chinatown is one of Canada's largest and most vibrant and is transforming at an even faster rate, hence is new condo blocks and hipster coffeeshops. These fascinating adjoining areas invite plenty of on-foot exploration.

The Sights in a Day

☀ Have your camera at the ready on Gastown's Water St and time your visit accordingly: the **Steam Clock** (p53) is Vancouver's most popular free attraction and it marks every quarter-hour with a tooting display from its steam pipes (the extended hourly display is best). Spend some time exploring the independent boutiques in this heritage-designated neighborhood, then doff your hat to Maple Tree Square's jaunty **Gassy Jack Statue** (p53) of the man who kick-started the 1800s city.

☀ Adjacent Chinatown is worth an afternoon of anyone's time. Start at the lofty **Chinatown Millennium Gate** (p51), peruse the old storefronts and newer boutiques and make note of possible dinner options. Then take a tranquility break at the delightful **Dr Sun Yat-Sen Classical Chinese Garden** (p48). Lunch? Try **Phnom Penh** (p55).

🌙 Visit the **Vancouver Police Museum** (p46) before it closes for the day, then snag a craft beer at the beloved **Alibi Room** (p56). When it's time for dinner, retrun to the heart of Gastown and join the coolsters at delicious **Tacofino** (p54).

For a local's day in Chinatown, see p50.

👁 Top Sights

Vancouver Police Museum (p46)

Dr Sun Yat-Sen Classical Chinese Garden & Park (p48)

🔍 Local Life

Chinatown Culture & History Crawl (p50)

💜 Best of Vancouver

Eating

Tacofino (p54)

Ask for Luigi (p54)

Drinking

Alibi Room (p56)

Diamond (p58)

Shopping

Eastside Flea (p60)

Community Thrift & Vintage (p60)

Getting There

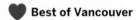

🚈 **Train** SkyTrain's Waterfront Station and Stadium-Chinatown Station service the area.

🚌 **Bus** Bus 14 heads from downtown along Hastings, handy for both Gastown and Chinatown. Buses 3, 4 and 8 also cover the area.

Top Sights
Vancouver Police Museum

The city's best hidden-gem museum does a
great job of poking at the seedy underbelly of
Vancouver's not-too-distant past. It's located in a
heritage brick building that formerly housed the
local coroner's court and its autopsy room (more
on that later). Head upstairs here and check your
nervous disposition at the entrance.

Morgue

The museum's first few exhibits explore the
history and heritage of Vancouver's police force.
You'll find grainy photos, framed badges and

◉ Map p52, E3

☎ 604-665-3346

www.vancouverpolicemuseum.ca

240 E Cordova St

adult/child $12/8

🕑 9am-5pm Tue-Sat

🚌 4

Milkshake Murder
July 1965

The Death Penalty
in British Columbia

mannequins wearing dusty uniforms. But, as you move through the rooms, the displays take on a darker hue until, suddenly, you find yourself in the autopsy room. Decommissioned in 1980 but almost unchanged since (which is why it's often used for film productions), the twin stainless-steel dissection tables here are a stark reminder of this room's grisly-but-essential purpose. If you're not convinced, peruse the slivers of human tissue (some with bullet holes) preserved on the walls. Then grab a toe-tag T-shirt from the gift shop to add your visit.

Crime Cases

Just before the spine-chilling autopsy room, look out for the row of tall glass display cases, each filled with an intriguing assortment of photos, exhibits and a skull or two. Each cabinet illuminates the story behind a notorious, sometimes unsolved crime from Vancouver's past. No punches are pulled – some crime-scene photos depict huge pools of blood – but it's well worth taking the time to carefully read the stories and connect to some hair-raising real-life tales that some Vancouverites can still recall firsthand.

Tooled-up

One of the museum's smaller rooms contains some wall-mounted display cases bristling with confiscated, often makeshift weapons found or seized around the city. It's a sobering array of spikes, chains, belts and razor-sharp shivs that wouldn't be out of place in a *Mad Max* movie. Many were created to be concealed and brought out by the perp whenever needed – and to cause maximum bone-crushing or skin-flailing damage (or both).

☑ Top Tips

▶ If you're here sometime between September and May, catch a monthly evening movie screening in the morgue – if you dare.

▶ Traveling with kids in summer? Book them in for a three-day **CSI Kids Camp**, complete with forensic investigation training.

▶ Toy car fan? Check out the almost hidden display of model police cars from around the world, tucked into a side room.

▶ Need more? The gift shop's related books include *The Last Gang in Town: The Epic Story of the Police vs. the Clark Park Gang*.

✕ Take a Break

▶ You're just a few steps from Railtown here, where the locals congregate over great pasta dishes at Ask for Luigi (p54).

Top Sights
Dr Sun Yat-Sen Classical Chinese Garden & Park

Reputedly the first Chinese 'scholars garden' ever built outside China and opened just in time for Vancouver's Expo '86 world exposition, this delightful oasis of tranquility is one of the city's most beloved ornamental green spaces. Framed by tile-topped whitewashed walls and centered on a mirror-calm pond fringed by twisting trees, its covered walkways are a sigh-triggering respite from clamorous Chinatown.

◉ Map p52, D4

www.vancouverchinesegarden.com

578 Carrall St

adult/child $14/10

🕙 9:30am-7pm mid-Jun–Aug, 10am-6pm Sep & May–mid-Jun, 10am-4:30pm Oct-Apr

Ⓢ Stadium-Chinatown

Harmonious Design

With symbol-heavy architecture that feels centuries old - walled courtyards, small bridges, flare-roof buildings and sidewalks fashioned from mosaics of patterned pebbles – this highly photogenic garden is also studded with large, eerie **limestone rocks** that look like they were imported from the moon. In reality, they were hauled all the way from Lake Tai in China. They give the garden a mystical, almost other-worldly feel.

Natural Jewels

The garden's large, lily-pad-covered **pond** is often as calm as a sheet of green glass – except when its resident neon-orange koi carp break the surface in hopes of snagging food from passers-by (don't feed them, though). They're not the only critters that call this watery haven home. Look carefully at some of the rocks poking from the water and you'll spot dozing turtles basking in the sun. Ducks, frogs and beady-eyed herons are also frequently spotted. Plant-wise, you'll find pine, bamboo, flowering plum trees and pots of decades-old bonsai trees that look like the diminutive offspring of Ents.

Summer Concerts

The **free guided tours** are a great way to unravel the symbolism behind the garden's features. But one of the best ways to immerse yourself further is via the summertime **Enchanted Evenings Concert Series**. Book ahead for these Thursday alfresco shows, which typically run in July and August, and you'll catch a sunset over the garden with a live music accompaniment. The eclectic roster of performers often runs from jazz to blues and choral to classical Chinese.

☑ Top Tips

▶ Arrive early on summer days to experience the garden's tranquility before the crowds roll in.

▶ Tours run hourly during the summer peak, but also several times a day throughout the rest of the year. Check the website schedule and time your visit accordingly.

▶ Peruse the gift shop before you leave; it's well-stocked with tea and traditional calligraphy tools.

▶ The towering Chinatown Millennium Gate is one block away if you still have some battery power left in your camera.

✕ Take a Break

Mix up your cultures with a German-style currywurst at Bestie (p55) on E Pender St.

Nearby Sai Woo (p55) is perfect for cocktails and soy ginger chicken.

Local Life
Chinatown Culture & History Crawl

One of North America's largest and most historic Chinatown districts, this heritage-designated Vancouver neighborhood has lots of stories to tell. Keep your camera handy and make sure to look above the storefront level here: the upper floors of many of Chinatown buildings have changed little in over a century.

❶ Photograph the Jack Chow Building

Once in the *Guinness Book of World Records* as the planet's narrowest commercial building, this slender **office site** (p54) resulted from a strange argument. Vancouverite Chang Toy owned the land but in 1926 all but a 1.8m-wide strip was expropriated by the city. Toy's revenge? He created this arms-wide building on what was left.

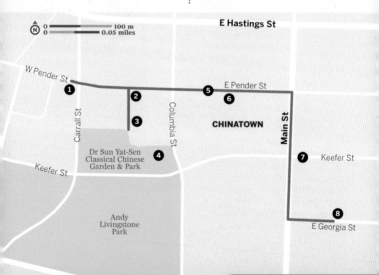

2 The Other Chinatown Gate

You'll have spotted the towering **Chinatown Millennium Gate** (p54) nearby but this ghostly white, much smaller one is also worth a photo or two. Originally fronting the Chinese pavilion at Vancouver's Expo '86, it was transplanted here after the event but soon began to crumble.

3 Peruse the Memorial Bronze

Behind the gate there's a paved plaza but the walkway leading to it has an intriguing bronze memorial set into its bright red tiles. It commemorates the historic contribution of Chinese workers to building Canada's nation-defining railway system.

4 Nose Around Sun Yat-Sen Park

The entrance to the popular **Dr Sun Yat-Sen Classical Chinese Garden** (p48) is here but this free-entry park alternative is also worth a look. With similar Chinese-themed nature-fringed walkways, a glassy-calm pond and a flare-roofed pavilion, it's a picturesque respite from Chinatown's busy streets.

5 Browse E Pender St Stores

The heart of Chinatown is lined with grocery and apothecary shops that have been serving the locals for decades. Newer, some would say gentrifying, business have also started popping up, including coffeeshops, hipster eateries and vintage stores.

6 Snack Stop at New Town Bakery

If you're hungry now, peruse the goodies at this historic Chinatown **fixture** (p56), including prawn turnovers and barbecued pork steamed buns.

7 Buckets of Frogs on Keefer

One of the neighborhood's most traditional streets, Keefer is crammed with family-run Chinese grocery stores, many of them hawking piles of unusual veggies, dried fish and the occasional bucket of live amphibians from their street side stands.

8 Dinner at Ramen Butcher

Many younger Chinese have moved to the city suburb of Richmond in the last couple of decades, leading some to predict the demise of Vancouver's historic Chinatown. But new businesses have now started popping up here again, including the first North American foray of this Japanese **franchise** (p55).

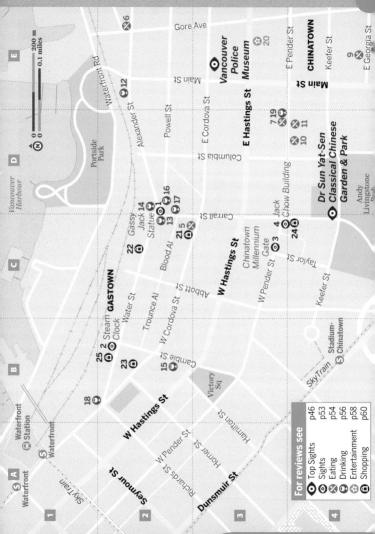

Vancouver Harbour

GASTOWN

Steam Clock

Victory Sq

W Hastings St

CHINATOWN

Vancouver Police Museum

Chinatown Millennium Gate

Dr Sun Yat-Sen Classical Chinese Garden & Park

Chow Building

Andy Livingstone Park

Stadium-Chinatown

Waterfront Station

Gore Ave

200 m
0.1 miles

SERJIO74/SHUTTERSTOCK ©

Steam Clock

Sights

Gassy Jack Statue   MONUMENT

1 ⊙ Map p52, D2

It's amusing to think that Vancouver's favorite statue is a testament to the virtues of drink. At least that's one interpretation of the John 'Gassy Jack' Deighton bronze, perched atop a whiskey barrel here in Maple Tree Sq. Erected in 1970, it recalls the time when Deighton arrived here in 1867 and built a pub, triggering a development that soon became Vancouver. (Maple Tree Sq; ☒4)

Steam Clock   LANDMARK

2 ⊙ Map p52, B2

Halfway along Water St, this oddly popular tourist magnet lures the cameras with its tooting steam whistle. Built in 1977, the clock's mechanism is actually driven by electricity; only the pipes on top are fueled by steam (reveal that to the patiently waiting tourists and you might cause a riot). It sounds every 15 minutes, and marks each hour with little whistling symphonies. (cnr Water & Cambie Sts; Ⓢ Waterfront)

Chinatown Millennium Gate

LANDMARK

 3 Map p52, C3

Inaugurated by Canadian prime minister Jean Chrétien in 2002, Chinatown's towering entrance is the landmark most visitors look for. Stand well back, since the decoration is mostly on its lofty upper reaches, an elaborately painted section that is topped with a terra-cotta-tiled roof. The characters that are inscribed on its eastern front implore you to 'Remember the past and look forward to the future.' (cnr W Pender & Taylor Sts; **S** Stadium-Chinatown)

Top Tip
Freebie Alternative Garden

Located right next door to the paid-entry Dr Sun Yat-Sen Classical Chinese Garden (p48), there's a fancy-free gratis alternative that shares some of its sibling's classical features. The **Dr Sun Yat-Sen Park** was inspired by the adjoining attraction and shares the same pond. It also has nature-fringed walkways that are encircled by tile-topped walls and its main feature is a small, red-roofed, Chinese-style pavilion that makes for great photos, especially when you catch it reflected off the pond.

Jack Chow Building

NOTABLE BUILDING

4 Map p52, C3

This spot, known for decades as the Sam Kee Building until Jack Chow Insurance changed the name and spruced it up, has been listed in the *Guinness Book of World Records* as the planet's shallowest commercial building. The new approach includes a Vegas-like musical light show on the outside of the structure. (www.jackchow.com; 8 W Pender St; **S** Stadium-Chinatown)

Eating

Tacofino

MEXICAN $

5 Map p52, C2

Food-truck favorite Tacofino made an instant splash with this huge, handsome dining room (think stylish geometric-patterned floors and hive-like lampshades). The simple menu focuses on a handful of taco options (six at lunch, more at dinner), plus nachos, soups and a selection of beer, agave and naughty tequila flights. Fish tacos are the top seller, but we love the super-tender lamb *birria* (stew). (☏604-899-7907; www.tacofino.com; 15 W Cordova St; tacos $6-12; ☐14)

Ask for Luigi

ITALIAN $$$

6 Map p52, E2

Consider an off-peak lunch if you don't want to wait too long for a table at this white-clapboard, shack-look little charmer (reservations are not accepted). Inside, you'll find a checkerboard floor and teak-lined interior crammed with tables and delighted diners tucking into (and sharing) plates of scratch-made pasta that mama never used to make; think bison tagliatelle and borage-and-ricotta ravioli. (☏604-428-2544; www.askforluigi.com; 305 Alexander St; mains $22-24; ☺11:30am-2:30pm & 5:30-10:30pm Tue-Fri, to 11pm Sat, to 9:30pm Sun; 🚌4)

Bestie GERMAN $

7 Map p52, D3

Like a food truck with a permanent home, this white-walled hole-in-the-wall specializes in Berlin-style curry-wursts – hearty sausages slathered in curry sauce, served with crunchy fries. It's popular with passing hipsters, so arrive off-peak for a chance of snagging the little cubby-hole window table: the best in the house. There's always a small but well-curated array of local craft beers to add to the fun. (☏604-620-1175; www.bestie.ca; 105 E Pender St; mains $4-11; ☺11:30am-10pm Sun-Thu, to midnight Fri & Sat; 📶; 🚌3)

Phnom Penh VIETNAMESE/CAMBODIAN $$

8 Map p52, E4

The dishes at this bustling joint are split between Cambodian and Vietnamese soul-food classics. It's the highly addictive chicken wings and their lovely pepper sauce that keep

regulars loyal. Once you've piled up the bones, dive back in for round two: papaya salad, butter beef and spring rolls show just how good a street-food-inspired Asian menu can be. (☏603-682-5777; 244 E Georgia St; mains $8-18; ☺10am-9pm Mon-Thu, to 11pm Fri-Sun; 🚌3)

Ramen Butcher RAMEN $

9 Map p52, E4

One of several new Asian-themed restaurants arriving in Chinatown in recent years, this is the first North American foray of a well-known Japanese ramen franchise. The signature thin noodles come in several broth-bowl varieties with slabs of slow-cooked pork; we recommend the garlicky Red Ramen. Still have some soup in your bowl? They'll toss in a second serving of noodles for free. (☏604-806-4646; www.theramenbutcher.com; 223 E Georgia St; mains $10-12; ☺11am-3pm & 5-10pm Tue-Thu, 11am-10pm Fri-Sun; 🚌3)

Sai Woo ASIAN $$

10 Map p52, D4

There's a film-set look to the exterior of this new eatery that makes it feel like a replica of an old Asian restaurant. But the lon interior is a great candlelit cave with a loungelike vibe. You'll find fusion dishes such as chop suey and soy-flavored ginger chicken; consider the 4:30pm-to-6pm happy hour with $6 dim sum specials and $5 beer and wine deals. (☏604-568-1117; www.saiwoo.ca; 158 E Pender; mains $12-18; ☺4:30pm-midnight Tue-Sat, 11am-3pm Sun; 🚌3)

New Town Bakery & Restaurant
CHINESE $

11 Map p52, D4

It's the glass cabinets of baked treats that lure most people through the door of this longtime Chinatown fixture; pop in for a well-priced prawn turnover or barbecued pork steamed bun to go. The takeout is the point of this place but if you're hungry for more, snag a table in the busy dining area at the back and dive into dim sum. (604-689-7835; www.newtownbakery.ca; 148 E Pender St; dishes $8-15; 6:30am-8:30pm; ; 3)

Drinking

Alibi Room
PUB

12 Map p52, E2

Vancouver's best craft-beer tavern has an exposed-brick bar that stocks an interesting roster of around 50 drafts, mostly from celebrated BC breweries such as Driftwood, Four Winds and Yellow Dog. Adventurous taste-trippers – hipsters and veteran beer fans alike – enjoy the $11.50 'frat bat' of four samples: choose your own or ask to be surprised. Check the board for ever-changing guest casks. (604-623-3383; www.alibi.ca; 157 Alexander St; 5-11:30pm Mon-Thu, 5pm-12:30am Fri, 10am-12:30am Sat, 10am-11:30pm Sun; ; 4)

Six Acres
BAR

13 Map p52, C2

Gastown's coziest tavern: you can cover all the necessary food groups via the carefully chosen draft- and bottled-beer list here. There's a small, animated summer patio out front but inside (especially upstairs) is great for hiding in a chatty, candlelit corner and working your way through the brews – plus a shared small plate or three (sausage board recommended). (604-488-0110; www.sixacres.ca; 203 Carrall St; 11:30am-11:30pm Sun-Thu, to 12:30am Fri & Sat; ; 4)

IV NIKOLNY/SHUTTERSTOCK ©

Gastown outdoor dining

Guilt & Co
BAR

14 Map p52, D2

This cavelike subterranean bar, beneath Gastown's brick-paved sidewalks, has a cult following among the kind of under-30s crowd that loves sipping Anchor Steam and playing Jenga at its tables (one of the many games available for imbibers to play). Avoid weekends when there are often line-ups and the place is crammed – drop by on a chilled-out weekday instead. (www.guiltandcompany.com; 1 Alexander St; ⏰7pm-late; Ⓢ Waterfront)

Revolver
COFFEE

15 Map p52, B2

With all those new hipster coffee shops opening around town, Revolver feels like an elder statesman, despite only being a few years old itself. It's remained at the top of the Vancouver coffee-mug tree via a serious commitment to great java. Aim for a little booth table or, if they're taken (they usually are), hit the large communal-table room next door. (☎604-558-4444; www.revolvercoffee.ca; 325 Cambie St; ⏰7:30am-6pm Mon-Fri, 9am-6pm Sat; 📶; 🚌14)

Diamond
COCKTAIL BAR

16 Map p52, D2

When you head upstairs via the unassuming entrance, you'll find yourself in one of Vancouver's warmest little cocktail bars. A renovated heritage room studded with sash windows – try for a view seat – it's popular with locals but is rarely pretentious. A list of perfectly nailed premium cocktails ($10 to $14) helps, coupled with a tapas menu that includes lots of Japanese-influenced options. (www.di6mond.com; 6 Powell St; ⏱5:30pm-1am Mon-Thu, to 2am Fri & Sat, to midnight Sun; 4)

Irish Heather
PUB

17 Map p52, D2

Belying the clichés about expat Irish bars (except for its reclaimed-Guinness-barrel floor), the Heather is one of Vancouver's best gastropubs. Alongside lovingly prepared sausage and mash, and steak-and-ale pie, you'll find good craft beers and, of course, some well-poured stout. Looking for happy hour? Drop by between 3pm and 6pm daily for $5 booze specials. (☏604-688-9779; www.irishheather.com; 210 Carrall St, Gastown; ⏱11:30am-midnight Sun-Thu, to 2am Fri & Sat; 🛜; 📷4)

Steamworks Brew Pub
BREWERY

18 Map p52, B1

This huge brewpub on the edge of Gastown serves several own-made beers, including pilsners, IPAs and pale ales. But the best of the bunch is the rich and velvety oatmeal stout. Popular with tourists and clocked-off office workers, Steamworks has an inviting pub-grub menu. Time your visit for the monthly Green Drinks night (www.greendrinks.org/bc/vancouver) when chatty enviro-types flirt with each other. (☏604-689-2739; www.steamworks.com; 375 Water St; ⏱11:30am-midnight Sun-Thu, to 1am Fri & Sat; Ⓢ Waterfront)

Fortune Sound Club
CLUB

19 Map p52, D3

Vancouver's best club has transformed a tired Chinatown spot into a slick space with the kind of genuine staff and younger, hipster-cool crowd rarely seen in Vancouver venues. Slide inside and you'll find a giant dance floor popping with party-loving locals just out for a good time. Expect weekend queues, and check out Happy Ending Fridays, when you'll possibly dance your ass off. (☏604-569-1758; www.fortunesoundclub.com; 147 E Pender St; ⏱9:30pm-3am Fri & Sat, plus special events; 📷3)

Entertainment

Rickshaw Theatre
LIVE MUSIC

20 Map p52, E3

Revamped from its grungy 1970s incarnation, the funky Rickshaw shows that Eastside gentrification can be positive. The stage of choice for many punk and indie acts, it's an

Understand

Vancouver's Oldest Street?

Great Fire

Just a few weeks after renaming itself Vancouver (no one liked the original name 'Granville,' nor the insalubrious 'Gastown' slang name that preceded it), in 1886 the fledgling city of around 1000 homes burnt almost to the ground in just minutes in what was termed the Great Fire. Within days, plans were drawn up for a new city. And this time, brick and stone would be favored over wood.

Starting Again

The first buildings radiated from Maple Tree Sq, in particular along Carrall St. This thoroughfare (also one of the shortest streets in Vancouver) still exists and it links the historic center of Gastown to Chinatown. Take a stroll south along Carrall and you'll spot some grand buildings from the city's early days. Perhaps due to an abundance of caution, they are some of the sturdiest structures around and will likely survive for many years to come, whether or not there's another fire.

Saving Gastown

If you'd visited 30 years ago, you would have seen many of these buildings seemingly on their last legs. This part of Vancouver hadn't attracted any new development or investment for years and Carrall St's paint-peeled taverns, hotels and storefronts were spiraling into skid row degradation. Two things changed the inevitable: heritage fans banded together to draw attention to the area's important role in the founding years of the city, a campaign that finally culminated in a national historic site designation in 2010. Secondly, gentrification arrived.

Upside of Grentrification?

With few neighborhoods around the city still left to enhance, the developers finally came back to the Downtown Eastside. While gentrification has many vocal detractors in this area, an undeniable positive is that it has preserved and protected Gastown's historic buildings for decades to come. The brick and stone landmarks that once lined Carrall have, for the most part, been sympathetically restored, giving the area an exciting new lease on life.

excellent place to see a band. It has a huge mosh area near the stage and rows of theater-style seats at the back. (☎604-681-8915; www.liveatrickshaw.com; 254 E Hastings St; 🚌14)

Shopping

Community Thrift & Vintage
VINTAGE

21 🔒 Map p52, C2

There are two branches of this popular vintage clothing store just around the corner from each other. This one focuses on clothes for men and women, while the other (311 Carrall St) is dedicated to womenswear and is lined with dresses from every conceivable era. Here, though, you'll find

---

⊙ Local Life
Hipster Market

Running for years at halls around the city, the monthly **Eastside Flea** (www.eastsideflea.com; Ellis Building, 1014 Main St; $3; ⊙6-10pm Fri, 11am-5pm Sat & Sun, 3rd weekend of the month; 🚌3) moved into its own permanent Ellis Building location in 2016. The renovated venue delivers 50 new and vintage vendors plus food trucks, live music and a highly inviting atmosphere. Arrive early so you can buy a top hat and swan around like the ironic out-of-time Victorian gentleman you've always wanted to be (bring your own waxed mustache).

---

shoes, tops and more to give your look that quirky retro lift you need. (☎604-682-1004; www.communitythriftandvintage.ca; 41 W Cordova St; ⊙11am-7pm Mon-Sat, noon-5pm Sun; 🚌14)

John Fluevog Shoes
SHOES

22 🔒 Map p52, C2

Like an art gallery for shoes, this alluringly cavernous store showcases the famed footwear of local designer Fluevog, whose men's and women's boots and brogues are what Doc Martens would have become if they'd stayed interesting and cutting-edge. Pick up that pair of thigh-hugging dominatrix boots you've always wanted or settle on some designer loafers that would make anyone walk tall. (☎604-688-6228; www.fluevog.com; 65 Water St; ⊙10am-7pm Mon-Wed & Sat, to 8pm Thu & Fri, noon-6pm Sun; Ⓢ Waterfront)

Salmagundi West
VINTAGE

23 🔒 Map p52, B2

For that one stubborn person on your souvenir list who defies the usual salmon or maple cookies gifts from Canada, try this beloved local gem: a browser's paradise. You'll find everything from reproduction old-school toys to oddly alluring taxidermy and sparkling Edwardian-style jewelry. There's a mix of old and new (but old-looking) and it's easy to spend a rainy hour or so digging in. (☎604-681-4648; 321 W Cordova St; ⊙11am-6pm Mon-Sat, noon-5pm Sun; Ⓢ Waterfront)

Water St, Gastown

Erin Templeton
FASHION & ACCESSORIES

24 Map p52, C4

Known for recycling leather into hip,
super-supple bags, belts, hats and
purses, this eponymous store has a
cult following. Erin herself is often
on hand and happy to chat about her
creations (she trained in shoemaking
at a London college). They're the kind
of must-have, one-of-a-kind items
that are hard to resist, no matter how
many bags you already have back
home. (604-682-2451; www.erintempleton.
com; 511 Carrall St; 11am-6pm Wed-Sat;
Stadium-Chinatown)

Coastal Peoples Fine Arts Gallery
ARTS & CRAFTS

25 Map p52, B2

This museumlike store showcases an
excellent array of Inuit and Northwest
Coast aboriginal jewelry, carvings and
prints. On the high-art side of things,
the exquisite items here are ideal if
you're looking for a very special souvenir for someone back home. Don't
worry: the gallery can ship the totem
poles if you can't fit them in your suitcase. (604-684-9222; www.coastal
peoples.com; 312 Water St; 10am-7pm
mid-Apr–mid-Oct, to 6pm mid-Oct–mid-Apr;
Waterfront)

Explore

Yaletown & Granville Island

Straddling False Creek, these opposite shoreline neighborhoods exemplify Vancouver's development in recent decades. A former rail-yard warehouse district, Yaletown is lined with chic restaurants and boutiques. Across the water, Granville Island was a grungy industrial area before being transformed in the 1970s into a haven of theaters, artisan studios and the best public market in Western Canada.

The Sights in a Day

☼ Kick off your day at **BC Place** (p72), the city's main sports stadium and home of the **Vancouver Whitecaps** (p78) soccer team and **BC Lions** (p78) Canadian Football League team. The stadium's **BC Sports Hall of Fame & Museum** (p72) is crammed with intriguing artifacts illuminating the region's sporting history.

☼ Drop in for lunch at Yaletown's **Flying Pig** (p75) then check out the chichi shops on the surrounding streets. This is Vancouver's version of Soho and the heritage brick-built warehouses are now filled with cool boutiques and restaurants. The area's history hasn't been completely forgotten, though: the **Engine 374 Pavilion** (p72) houses the locomotive that pulled the first transcontinental passenger train into Vancouver in 1887.

☾ Hop on a miniferry for a Granville Island night out. Aim for fish and chips at **Tony's Fish & Oyster Cafe** (p75), sip cocktails at **Liberty Distillery** (p65) and then catch a play at the **Granville Island Stage** (p79). If you're still up for fun, consider a late-night improv show at **Vancouver Theatresports League** (p79).

For a local's day on Granville Island, see p68.

 Top Sights

Granville Island Public Market (p64)

🔍 **Local Life**

Off-the-beaten-path Granville Island (p68)

❤ **Best of Vancouver**

Eating

Bistro 101 (p76)

Tony's Fish & Oyster Cafe (p75)

Drinking

Liberty Distillery (p65)

Artisan Sake Maker (p76)

Shopping

Gallery of BC Ceramics (p79)

Crafthouse (p69)

Getting There

🚌 **Bus** Number 50 stops near Granville Island's entrance; 10 on Granville Bridge's south side – a five-minute stroll under the island.

🚃 **Train** The Canada Line stops at Yaletown-Roundhouse Station.

⚓ **Miniferries** Granville Island and Yaletown are connected by miniferries.

Top Sights
Granville Island Public Market

A foodie extravaganza specializing in deli treats and pyramids of shiny fruit and vegetables, this is one of North America's finest public markets. It's ideal for whiling away an afternoon, snacking on goodies in the sun among the buskers outside or avoiding the rain with a market tour. You'll also find side dishes of (admittedly nonedible) arts and crafts.

👁 Map p70, B3

📞 604-666-6655

www.granvilleisland.com/public-market

Johnston St

🕘 9am-7pm

🚌 50, ⛴ miniferries

Taste-tripping

Come hungry: there are dozens of food stands to weave your way around at the market. Among the must-see stands are **Oyama Sausage Company**, replete with hundreds of smoked sausages and cured meats; **Benton Brothers Fine Cheese**, with its full complement of amazing curdy goodies from British Columbia (BC) and around the world (look for anything by Farm House Natural Cheese from Agassiz, BC); and **Granville Island Tea Company** (Hawaiian rooibos recommended), with its tasting bar and more than 150 steep-tastic varieties to choose from. Baked goodies also abound: abandon your diet at **Lee's Donuts** and **Siegel's Bagels**, where the naughty cheese-stuffed baked bagels are not to be missed. And don't worry; there's always room for a wafer-thin album-sized 'cinnamon record' from **Stuart's Baked Goods**.

French-themed **L'Epicerie Rotisserie and Gourmet Shop** has also been a popular addition to the market in recent years. It sells vinegars, olive oils and Babapapa pop bottles with delicious, freshly cooked picnic-friendly takeout chicken and sausages.

Arts & Crafts

Once you've eaten your fill, take a look at some of the market's other stands. There's a cool arts and crafts focus here, especially among the collection of **day vendors** that dot the market and which change every week. Hand-knitted hats, hand-painted ceramics, framed art photography and quirky carvings will make for excellent one-of-a-kind souvenirs – far better than the typical canned salmon and maple-sugar cookies. Further artisan stands are added to the roster in the run-up to Christmas, if you happen to be here at that time. For more information on the sorts of day vendors that appear at the market, visit www.gidva.org.

☑ Top Tips

▶ In summer, arrive early to sidestep the crowds, which peak in the afternoons.

▶ If you're driving, weekdays are the easiest times to find on-island parking.

▶ The food court is the island's best-value dining but tables are scarce at peak times.

▶ A visiting birdwatcher? Look for the cormorants nesting under the Granville Bridge span.

▶ Gather a great picnic, then find a quiet spot to dine; the grassy knoll at the island's opposite end is ideal.

✗ Take a Break

▶ A short stroll from the Public Market, **Liberty Distillery** (p78) is one of the region's best craft gin and vodka producers.

▶ On Railspur Alley is the hidden gem Artisan Sake Maker (p76), which crafts smooth versions of the traditional Japanese tipple.

A great selection of fresh produce for sale

Understand
Granville Island's Industrial Edge

- -

One million cubic yards of landfill was tipped into False Creek to create Granville Island in the early 20th century, but almost all the reminders of its gritty first few years have been lost. Almost. The area's oldest tenant, Ocean Concrete, is a cement maker that began here in 1917 and now cranks out enough product to build a 10-story tower block every week. It also does a great job of being a good neighbor. A recent Vancouver Biennale initiative saw the company's six gigantic waterfront silos transformed into huge painted figures, and its annual April open house event is hotly anticipated by local families.

Continue along Johnston a little further – noticing the disused old rail lines still embedded in the island's roads – and you'll come to a second monument to the past: a landmark yellow dock crane that's been preserved from the old days. Nip across to the waterfront here for a final 'hidden' Granville Island view: some large and comfy-looking houseboats that many Vancouverites wish they lived in.

Insider's Tour

If you're an incurable foodie, the delicious market tour organized by Vancouver Foodie Tours is the way to go. Taking about two hours to weave around the vendors and costing from $50, the morning-only guided amble includes tastings of regional foods and chef-approved tips on how to pair and prepare local ingredients. It caters to vegetarians if you ask when you book and there's also a $10 discount for epicurious children (aged 3 to 12). The company also runs culinary tours in other parts of the city if you're keen to keep eating; the Vancouver food truck tour is especially popular.

Forgotten Past

The Public Market is the centerpiece of one of Canada's most impressive urban regeneration projects – and the main reason it has been so successful. Built as a district for small factories in the early part of the last century, Granville Island – which has also been called Mud Island and Industrial Island over the years – had declined into a paint-peeled, no-go area by the 1960s. But the abandoned sheds began attracting artists and

> ### Understand
> ### Twin Bridges
>
> If you're out enjoying the buskers on the market's waterfront exterior, you'll notice your False Creek view is sandwiched between two of Vancouver's most famous bridges. Opened in 1954, the ironwork Granville Bridge is the third version of this bridge to span the inlet here. The more attractive art deco Burrard Bridge, opened in 1932, is nearby. During its opening ceremony, a floatplane was daringly piloted under the bridge's main deck.

theater groups by the 1970s, and the old buildings slowly started springing back to life with some much-needed repairs and upgrades. Within a few years, new theaters, restaurants and studios had been built and the Public Market quickly became an instantly popular anchor tenant. One reason for the island's popularity? Only independent, one-of-a-kind businesses operate here.

Local Life
Off-the-beaten-path Granville Island

Most visitors head straight for the Public Market but locals know there's much more to check out on this artificial island, built up from a pair of sandbanks in False Creek more than a century ago. Originally an industrial district, it was reinvented as an arts and crafts hub in the 1970s and is perfect for on-foot exploration.

❶ Prepare for Rain at the Umbrella Shop

Head to this historic **shop** (p80) to buy a sturdy brolly - an essential item for Vancouver's frequently rainy weather.

❷ Check out the Kids Market

This wonderful double-story **market** (p73) offers 25 children's stores ranging from all kinds of toys to crafts and even magic tricks.

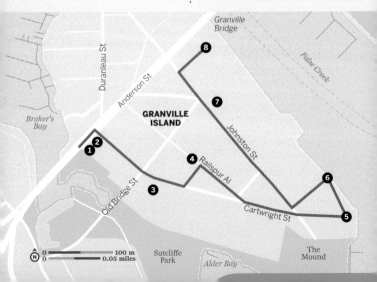

3 Get Crafty at the Crafthouse
A friendly nonprofit **gallery** (p81) run by the Craft Council of British Columbia (CCBC), showcasing a wide range of textiles and homewares all produced by local artisans.

4 Amble Along Railspur Alley
Seemingly far from the madding crowds of the Public Market – at least on days when every tourist in town seems to be there – this back-alley strip is a relaxing alternative. There's a string of artisan stores and even a sake producer if you need a boozy pit stop.

5 Beer on the Patio at Dockside
At Granville Island's quieter end, grab a waterfront seat at **Dockside** (p78) and try its excellent housemade beers.

6 Houseboat Spotting
A clutch of lucky Vancouverites live on this end of the island in a double row of large, flower-covered houseboats guaranteed to trigger a little home envy. There are also some reminders of the island's gritty industrial past here; look out for the preserved yellow-painted dock crane plus the disused rail lines striping the sidewalks.

7 Quick Ocean Concrete Stop
The most obvious reminder of the time when this was locally known as Industrial Island, the area's oldest tenant started here in 1917. The concrete producer now makes enough product to build a 10-storey tower every week. Check the cool kinetic artwork installation out front and aim for April's family-friendly open house.

8 Duck into the Silk Weaving Studio
This labyrinthine complex under Granville Bridge is a local crafting **favorite** (p81) that features enticing displays of silk threads available in every color under the sun.

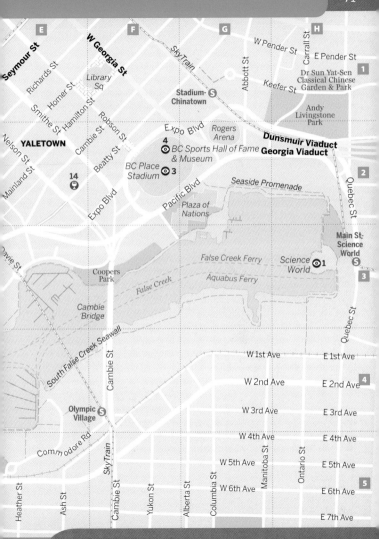

E

Seymour St

Richards St

Homer St

Smithe St

Hamilton St

Nelson St

YALETOWN

Cambie St

Mainland St

F

W Georgia St

Library Sq

Robson St

Beatty St

Expo Blvd

14

G

SkyTrain

Abbott St

Stadium-Chinatown S

Expo Blvd

4

BC Sports Hall of Fame
& Museum

Rogers Arena

BC Place Stadium 3

Pacific Blvd

Plaza of Nations

W Pender St

Carrall St

H

E Pender St

Keefer St

Dr Sun Yat-Sen
Classical Chinese
Garden & Park

1

Andy
Livingston
Park

Dunsmuir Viaduct
Georgia Viaduct

Quebec St

2

Seaside Promenade

Davie St

Coopers
Park

Cambie
Bridge

South False Creek Seawall

Olympic
Village S

Commodore Rd

Heather St

Ash St

Cambie St

SkyTrain

Yukon St

Alberta St

False Creek

False Creek Ferry

Aquabus Ferry

Columbia St

W 1st Ave

W 2nd Ave

W 3rd Ave

W 4th Ave

W 5th Ave

W 6th Ave

Science
World 1

Manitoba St

Ontario St

Main St-
Science
World S

3

E 1st Ave

E 2nd Ave

E 3rd Ave

E 4th Ave

E 5th Ave

E 6th Ave

E 7th Ave

Quebec St

4

5

Sights

Science World
MUSEUM

1 Map p70, H3

Under Vancouver's favorite geodesic dome (okay, its only one), this ever-popular science and nature showcase has tons of exhibition space and a cool outdoor park crammed with hands-on fun (yes, you *can* lift 2028kg). Inside, there are two floors of educational play, from a walk-in hamster wheel to an air-driven ball maze. (☏604-443-7440; www.scienceworld.ca; 1455 Quebec St; adult/child $25.75/17.75; ⏱10am-6pm, to 8pm Thu Jul & Aug, reduced hours off-season; P🚼; SMain St-Science World)

Engine 374 Pavilion
MUSEUM

2 Map p70, D3

May 23, 1887, was an auspicious date for Vancouver. That's when Engine 374 pulled the very first transcontinental passenger train into the fledgling city, symbolically linking the country and kick-starting the eventual metropolis. Retired in 1945, the engine was, after many years of neglect, restored and placed in this splendid pavilion. The friendly volunteers here will show you the best angle for snapping the perfect photo of the engine. (www.roundhouse.ca; Roundhouse Community Arts & Recreation Centre, 181 Roundhouse Mews; admission free; ⏱10am-4pm, reduced hours off-season; 🚼; SYaletown-Roundhouse)

BC Place Stadium
STADIUM

3 Map p70, F2

Vancouver's main sports arena is home to two professional teams: the **BC Lions** Canadian Football League team (p78) and the **Vancouver Whitecaps** soccer team (p78). Also used for major rock concerts and consumer shows, the renovated stadium – with its huge, crown-like retractable roof – hosted the opening and closing ceremonies for the 2010 Olympic and Paralymic Winter Games. (☏604-669-2300; www.bcplacestadium.com; 777 Pacific Blvd; P; SStadium-Chinatown)

BC Sports Hall of Fame & Museum
MUSEUM

4 Map p70, F2

Inside BC Place Stadium, this small but perfectly formed attraction showcases top BC athletes, both amateur and professional, with galleries devoted to each decade in sports. There are medals, trophies and sporting memorabilia on display (judging by the size of their shirts, hockey players were much smaller in the old days), and tons of hands-on activities to tire the kids out. (☏604-687-5520; www.bcsportshalloffame.com; Gate A, BC Place Stadium, 777 Pacific Blvd; adult/child $15/12; ⏱10am-5pm; 🚼; SStadium-Chinatown)

LISSANDRA MELO/SHUTTERSTOCK ©

Science World

Ecomarine Paddlesport Centres

KAYAKING

5  Map p70, A3

Headquartered on Granville Island, Ecomarine offers kayak and stand-up paddleboard (SUP) rentals, plus popular guided tours around the area. At the center's **Jericho Beach branch** (1300 Discovery St, Jericho Sailing Centre; ⏰10am-dusk Mon-Fri, 9am-dusk Jun-Aug; 🚌4), events and seminars are organized where you can rub shoulders with local paddle nuts. They also arrange multiday tours around some of BC's most magical marine regions. (📞604-689-7575; www.eco marine.com; 1668 Duranleau St; kayak/paddle-board rental per 2hr $39/29; ⏰9am-9pm Jun & Jul, to 8pm Aug, 10am-6pm Sep-May; 🚌50)

Kids Market

MARKET

6 Map p70, A4

A nightmare if you stroll in by mistake, this two-story mini-shopping mall for under-10s is bustling with 25 kid-friendly stores, mostly of the toy variety. If your child's interests extend beyond Lego, there are also magic tricks, arts and crafts, and a menagerie of puppets for sale. Cool the sprogs down at the huge **Granville Island Water Park** (admission free; ⏰summer; 👶; 🚌50) out back. (📞604-689-8447; www.kidsmarket.ca; 1496 Cartwright St; ⏰10am-6pm; 👶; 🚌50)

Understand
Vancouver's Brick-built Soho

Railway Foundation

Aesthetically unlike any other Vancouver neighborhood, Yaletown has a trendy warehouse district appearance today because it was built on a foundation of grungy, working-class history. Created almost entirely from red bricks, the area was crammed with railway sheds and goods warehouses in the late 1800s after the Canadian Pacific Railway (CPR) relocated its main western Canada operation from the small BC town of Yale. The 'new Yale' was striped with rail lines and populated with lofty warehouses.

Neighborhood Decline

Along with the Yale moniker, the area's railway workers brought something else with them: a tough-as-nails approach that turned the waterfront area into one where the taverns served their liquor with a side order of fist-fights. But at least the workers kept the area alive: when the rail operations were closed down a few decades after moving here, Yaletown descended into a half-empty mass squat filled with homeless locals and marauding rats. The writing - or at least the district's demolition - seemed just a matter of time.

Resurrection

But that wasn't the end of Yaletown's story. When plans were announced for Vancouver to host the giant Expo '86 world exposition, there were few areas with the space – and the absence of other businesses – to host it. But half-empty Yaletown fit the bill. The neighborhood was swiftly chosen to be part of the planned Expo grounds along the north shoreline of False Creek. It was soon spruced up and given a new lease on life.

Post-Expo Polish

After the fair, Yaletown's newly noticed heritage character made it ideal for urban regeneration. Within a few years, the old brick warehouses had been repaired, scrubbed clean and recolonized with boutiques, fancy restaurants and swish bars – serving tipples a far cry from the punch-triggering beers that used to be downed here.

Eating

Tony's Fish & Oyster Cafe

SEAFOOD $$

7 ⊠ Map p70, A4

A chatty spot where Vancouverites bring visitors when they take them to Granville Island, this tiny checkered-tablecloth joint serves great fish and chips, along with generous dollops of housemade coleslaw and tartar sauce. The food is good value, and it's not just about fish and chips: the BBQ-sauced oyster burger is almost a local legend. Service is fast and friendly. (☎604-683-7127; www.tonysfishandoyster cafe.com; 1511 Anderson St; mains $9-25; ⊗11:30am-8:30pm, reduced hours in winter; ⊠50)

A Bread Affair

BAKERY $

8 ⊠ Map p70, A3

A fire a few years back didn't kill this beloved organic bakery; it rose phoe-nixlike from the burned breadcrumbs. Alongside its sandwich bar (French ham and Havarti recommended) and racks of fresh-baked loaves, there's an irresistible array of treats, from cookies to croissants. Don't miss the hearty apple-cheddar-walnut galette; it's enough to feed two but that doesn't mean you have to. (☎604-695-0000; www.abreadaffair.com; 1680 Johnston St; sandwiches $9-11; ⊗8:30am-7pm Mon-Thu, to 7:30pm Fri-Sun; ⊠50)

Edible Canada

CANADIAN $$

9 ⊠ Map p70, B3

Granville Island's most popular bistro (book ahead) delivers a short but tempting menu of seasonal dishes, mostly from BC but also from across Canada, often including ingredients such as elk tartare or Quebec cheeses. Consider sharing some small plates if you're feeling adventurous and also add a selection from the all-Canadian wine list (including an ice-wine finale). (☎604-682-6681; www.edible canada.com/bistro; 1596 Johnston St; mains $18-30; ⊗11am-9pm Mon-Fri, 9am-10pm Sat & Sun; ⊠50)

Flying Pig

CANADIAN $$

10 ⊠ Map p70, D2

Yaletown's best midrange restaurant is a warm, woodsy bistro that has mastered the art of friendly service and saliva-triggering, gourmet comfort food. Dishes focus on seasonal local ingredients and are virtually guaranteed to make your belly smile. Wine-braised short ribs and roast chicken served with buttermilk mash top our to-eat list, but it's best to arrive off-peak to avoid the crowds. (☎604-568-1344; www.theflyingpigvan.com; 1168 Hamilton St; mains $19-27; ⊗11am-midnight Mon-Fri, 10am-midnight Sat, 10am-11pm Sun; ⑤Yaletown-Roundhouse)

Go Fish
SEAFOOD $

11 ⊗ Map p70, A3

A short stroll westwards along the seawall from the Granville Island entrance, this almost-too-popular seafood stand is one the city's fave fish-and-chip joints, offering halibut, salmon and cod encased in crispy golden batter. The smashing (and lighter) fish tacos are also recommended, while the changing daily specials – brought in by the nearby fishing boats – often include scallop burgers or ahi tuna sandwiches. (☏604-730-5040; 1505 W 1st Ave; mains $8-14; ☺11:30am-6:30pm Mon-Fri, noon-6:30pm Sat & Sun; ☐50)

◯ Local Life
Gourmet Dining on a Budget

Vancouver's best-value gourmet dining option, **Bistro 101** (Map p70, A4; ☏604-724-4488; www.picachef. com; 1505 W 2nd Ave; ☺11:30am-2pm & 6-9pm Mon-Fri; ☐50) – the training restaurant of the **Pacific Institute of Culinary Arts** – is popular with in-the-know locals, especially at lunchtime when $22 gets you a delicious three-course meal (typically three options for each course) plus service that's earnestly solicitous. The dinner option costs $8 more and there's a buffet offering on the first Friday of the month. Reservations recommended.

Rodney's Oyster House
SEAFOOD $$

12 ⊗ Map p70, D3

Vancouver's favorite oyster eatery, Rodney's always has a buzz. And it's not just because of the convivial room with its nautical flourishes: these folks really know how to do seafood. While the fresh-shucked oysters with a huge array of sauces (try the spicy vodka) never fail to impress, everything from sweet mussels to superb Atlantic lobster is also available here. (☏604-609-0080; www.rohvan.com; 1228 Hamilton St; mains $16-32; ☺11:30am-11pm; ⑤Yaletown-Roundhouse)

Drinking

Artisan Sake Maker
BREWERY

13 ⌷ Map p70, B4

This tiny sake producer uses locally grown rice – making it the first of its kind in Canada – and should be on everyone's Granville Island to-do list. Twinkle-eyed sake maker Masa Shiroki produces several tipples and you can dive in for a bargain $5 three-sake tasting. It's an eye-opening revelation to many drinkers who think sake is a harsh beverage. Take-out bottles are available. (☏604-685-7253; www. artisansakemaker.com; 1339 Railspur Alley; ☺11:30am-6pm; ☐50)

Granville Island Brewing Taproom

Central City Brew Pub CRAFT BEER

14 Map p70, E2

Colonizing the site of former brewpub favorite Dix (that's their old sign on the wall inside), the downtown satellite of one of BC's most celebrated beermakers combines a passable pub-grub menu with a sparkling array of beers – its own as well as top picks from many other BC producers. Best Central City brews to try? Red Racer IPA and Red Racer India Red Ale. (☏778-379-2489; www.centralcitybrewing. com; 871 Beatty St; ☺11am-mdinight Sun-Thu, to 1am Fri & Sat; ☐17)

Granville Island Brewing Taproom PUB

15 Map p70, B4

You can sample the company's main beers in this pub-style room, although most are now made in a large out-of-town facility. Among these, Cypress Honey Lager, Lions Winter Ale and summertime False Creek Raspberry Ale are among the most popular. But the small-batch Black Notebook brews, made right here on the island, are even better: ask your server what's available. (☏604-687-2739; www.gib.ca; 1441 Cartwright St; ☺11am-9pm; ☐50)

Backstage Lounge BAR

This dark, under-the-bridge Granville Island hangout (see 17 ⭐ Map p70, B3) has winning patio views and frequent local-band live music playing. The bar is lined with more than 20 mostly BC microbrew taps from the likes of Driftwood, Phillips and Red Truck, and there is always a bargain $2.75 special running on Tuesdays and Thursdays from Bowen Island Brewing. The pub-grub food menu includes good flatbread pizzas. (📞604-687-1354; www.thebackstagelounge.com; 1585 Johnston St; 🕐noon-2am Mon-Sat, to midnight Sun; 🚌50)

Local Life
Granville Island's Best Happy Hour

Vancouver's most attractive craft distillery, **Liberty** (Map p70, B4; 📞604-558-1998; www.theliberty distillery.com; 1494 Old Bridge St; 🕐11am-8pm; 🚌50) has a handsome, saloon-style tasting room where you can gaze through windows at the shiny, steampunk-like booze-making equipment beyond. It's not all about looks, though. During the Monday-to-Thursday 3pm-to-6pm happy hour, you can sample onsite-made gin, vodka and white whiskey plus great cocktails for just $6 a pop. Tours are also available ($10; Saturdays and Sundays; 11:30am and 1:30pm).

Dockside Brewing Company BAR

16 Map p70, C4

Often overshadowed by the other brewers in town (being stuck on the quiet end of Granville Island doesn't help), Dockside's beers are made on site and include the tasty, hibiscus-toned Jamaican Lager. Sup on the excellent waterfront patio for tranquil views of False Creek's boat traffic and you may have to be forcibly removed by the end of the night. (📞604-685-7070; www.docksidebrewing.com; Granville Island Hotel, 1253 Johnston St; 🕐11:30am-10pm; 🚌50)

Entertainment

Vancouver Whitecaps SOCCER

Using BC Place Stadium (see 3 ◎ Map p70, F2) as its home, Vancouver's professional soccer team plays in North America's top-tier Major League Soccer (MLS). The team has struggled a little since being promoted to the league in 2011, but has been finding its feet (useful for soccer players) in recent seasons. Save time to buy a souvenir soccer shirt to impress everyone back home. (📞604-669-9283; www.whitecapsfc.com; BC Place Stadium, 777 Pacific Blvd; tickets $30-150; 🕐Mar-Oct; 🚶; Ⓢ Stadium-Chinatown)

BC Lions FOOTBALL

The Lions is Vancouver's team in the Canadian Football League (CFL), which is arguably more exciting than its US counterpart, the NFL. It's had some decent showings in recent years but hasn't won the all-important Grey Cup championship since 2011. Playing at BC Stadium (see 3 Map p70, F2), tickets are easy to come by – unless the boys are laying into their arch enemies, the Calgary Stampeders. (📞604-589-7627; www.bclions.com; BC Place Stadium, 777 Pacific Blvd; tickets from $35; ⊙Jun-Nov; 🚶; Ⓢ Stadium-Chinatown)

Granville Island Stage THEATER

17 ⭐ Map p70, B3

The Granville Island arm of Vancouver's leading theater company, this intimate, raked-seating venue is the perfect spot to feel really connected to the action on stage. Cutting-edge homegrown shows as well as new versions of established hits (especially blockbuster musicals in early summer) populate the season here and you're close to several restaurants if you fancy a dinner-and-a-show night out. (📞604-687-1644; www.artsclub.com; 1585 Johnston St; tickets from $29; ⊙Sep-Jun; 🚌50)

Vancouver Theatresports League COMEDY

18 ⭐ Map p70, A4

The city's most popular improv group stages energetic romps – sometimes connected to themes such as Shakespeare or *Game of Thrones* – at this purpose-fitted theater. Whatever the theme, the approach is the same: if you're sitting near the front, expect to be picked on. The 11:15pm Friday

✅ Top Tip

Theatrical Money-savers

Granville Island is the heart of Vancouver's theater scene and hosts several stages and festivals. See what's on and save money on shows here and throughout the city by checking the daily half-price deals at www.ticketstonight.ca. Alternatively, time your visit for September's **Vancouver Fringe Festival** (www.vancouverfringe.com; ⊙mid-Sep). Colonizing venues large and small throughout Granville island, it offers hundreds of shows, multiple genres and well-priced tickets. Passes are also available if you fancy catching a string of shows.

and Saturday shows are commendably ribald. Check www.ticketstonight.ca for same-day half-price tickets. (📞604-738-7013; www.vtsl.com; The Improv Centre, 1502 Duranleau St; tickets $15-22; ⊙Wed-Sun; 🚌50)

Shopping

Gallery of BC Ceramics ARTS & CRAFTS

19 🔒 Map p70, B4

The star of Granville Island's arts-and-crafts shops and the public face of the Potters Guild of BC, this excellent spot exhibits and sells the striking works of its member artists. You can pick up unique ceramic tankards or swirly-painted soup bowls; the hot items are

Silk Weaving Studio

books and well-priced animal-themed earrings (we like the bats and cat heads). (☏604-684-2534; www.paper-ya. com; 1666 Johnston St, Net Loft; ⊙10am-7pm; ☐50)

Xoxolat
CHOCOLATE

 21 Map p70, D2

Pronounced *sho-sho-la*, one of Vancouver's finest chocolate shops lured a whole new sticky-fingered audience when it moved from a tiny across-town spot a few years back. The larger space enabled it to increase its racks of top-notch gourmet chocolate bars from around the world as well as displaying more of its own-made truffles, slabs and signature chocolate shoes. (☏604-733-2462; www.xoxolat.com; 1271 Homer St; ⊙10:30am-6pm Tue-Sat, noon-5pm Sun & Mon; ⓢYaletown-Roundhouse)

the cool ramen-noodle cups, complete with holes for chopsticks. It's well-priced art for everyone. (☏604-669-3606; www.bcpotters.com; 1359 Cartwright St; ⊙10:30am-5:30pm; ☐50)

Paper-Ya
ARTS & CRAFTS

20 Map p70, A3

A magnet for slavering stationery fetishists (you know who you are), this store's treasure trove of trinkets ranges from natty pens to traditional washi paper. It's not all writing-related ephemera, though. Whoever does the buying also curates an eclectic, changing roster of hard-to-resist treats including cool watches, adult coloring

Umbrella Shop
FASHION & ACCESSORIES

 22 Map p70, A4

Perhaps the only outdoor gear you'll need in Vancouver is a sturdy brolly to fend off the relentless rain. This family-run company started in 1935 and has just the thing, with hundreds of bright and breezy designs that should put a smile on the face of any tempest-addled visitor. Duck inside, choose a great umbrella, then launch yourself back into the storm. (☏604-697-0919; www.theumbrellashop.com; 1550 Anderson St; ⊙10am-6pm; ☐50)

Silk Weaving Studio ARTS & CRAFTS

23 🔒 Map p70, B3

Almost hidden in a back alley maze of buildings, this beloved local favorite is a crafter's delight. It's hard not to stroke every strand of silk in sight, with a rainbow of colored threads and yarns calling your name. Watch out for weaving demonstrations. You'll find this store tucked down a nameless alley immediately under the bridge. (📞604-687-7455; www.silkweavingstudio.com; 1531 Johnston St; ⊙10am-5pm; 🚌50)

Crafthouse ARTS & CRAFTS

24 🔒 Map p70, B4

At this bright and friendly nonprofit gallery run by the Craft Council of British Columbia (CCBC), the shelves hold everything from glass goblets and woven scarves to French butter dishes and lathe-turned arbutus wood bowls – all produced by dozens of artisans from across the region. It's a great place to pick up something different for friends and family back home. (📞604-687-7270; www.craftcouncilbc.ca; 1386 Cartwright St; ⊙10am-6pm May-Aug, 10:30am-5:30pm Sep-Apr; 🚌50)

Cross HOMEWARES

25 🔒 Map p70, D2

Not everything is white at this large, high-ceilinged interior store but it certainly veers towards the pastel. From perfect wine glasses to cool linens, there's a continental, vintage-chic feel to the collection. It's ideal for a rainy-day browse, but be careful: you'll almost certainly find something you want to buy, which could mean blowing your baggage allowance on the way home. (📞604-689-2900; www.thecrossdesign.com; 1198 Homer St; ⊙10am-6pm Mon-Sat, 11am-5pm Sun; Ⓢ Yaletown-Roundhouse)

Local Life
Commercial Drive Drink & Dine

Vancouver's original counterculture neighborhood, today's Drive is a funky, strollable promenade of independent shops, one-of-a-kind restaurants and laid-back coffeehouses, many of them founded by the Italian immigrants who arrived here in the 1950s. Ideal for a relaxing afternoon with the locals, it's also well stocked with good bars and inviting, sun-dappled dining patios.

Getting There

🚇 Expo/Millennium Line from downtown to Commercial-Broadway station.

🚌 99B-Line express services and number 9 regular services stop at the Broadway and Commercial intersection.

1 Beers at St Augustine

Home to one of the city's biggest draft microbrew menus, **St Augustine's** (📞604-569-1911; www.staugustinesvancouver.com; 2360 Commercial Dr; ⏰11am-1am Sun-Thu, to 2am Fri & Sat; Ⓢ Commercial-Broadway) is a busy Vancouver tavern. Celebrate the patron saint of brewing by diving into the dozens of available ales; seasonals highly recommended.

2 Coffee at Prado

If you've slightly over-indulged, sober up with a strong coffee at this white-walled **java haunt** (📞604-255-5537; www.pradocafevancouver.com; 1938 Commercial Dr; ⏰7am-8pm Mon-Fri, 7am-7pm Sat, 8am-7pm Sun; 📶; 🚌20). One of the Drive's hippest coffee spots (plaid is like a dress code here), it's loved by MacBook-wielding regulars quietly updating their social media accounts.

3 Sunny Grandview Park Pit Stop

If it suddenly feels like snooze time, the Drive's favorite alfresco **hangout** (Commercial Dr, btwn Charles & William Sts; 🚌20) invites you to lie back in the grass and watch the clouds. But not before checking out the vistas to the north (those craggy-topped mountains) and west (downtown's twinkling towers).

4 Drink or Dine at Biercraft Tap & Tapas

This Euro-style **resto-bar** (📞604-254-2437; www.biercraft.com; 1191 Commercial Dr; ⏰11am-11:30pm Mon, Tue & Fri, 11am-midnight Wed & Thu, 10am-1pm Sat, 10am-11:30pm Sun; 🚌20) is one of the Drive's most popular. Play it safe with a slowly-sipped whiskey or faceplant into the amazing beer array, including strong tipples from Belgium. Even better, forsake the booze for a bowl of broth-tastic mussels.

5 Spicy Late Lunch at the Reef

If you didn't eat at Biercraft, this cheery **Caribbean restaurant** (📞604-568-5375; www.thereefrestaurant.com; 1018 Commercial Dr; mains $14-19; ⏰11am-10pm Mon-Fri, 10am-11pm Sat & Sun; 🚌20) is a great alternative, with a menu of nicely spiced soul food. Keen to stay on an even keel? The cocktails also come in nonalcoholic versions.

6 Snacks at the Licorice Parlour

A quirky **artisan candy store** (📞604-558-2422; 1002 Commercial Dr; ⏰11am-6pm; 🚌20) stocking imported varieties but also selling handmade hula-hoops (of course). Balance a hoop around your waist, snag some licorice to go and shimmy off along the street.

7 Dessert at Uprising Breads Bakery cafe

Don't miss the murals painted along the side streets on either side of you, then turn left onto Venables St for this smashing **bakery cafe** (📞604-254-5635; www.uprisingbreads.com; 1697 Venables St; mains $6-10; ⏰7am-7pm Mon-Fri, 7am-6pm Sat & Sun; 🚌20). Sit down with a coffee and cake and consider the dinner options you've passed along the Drive.

Local Life
Main Street Hipster Stroll

The skinny-jeaned heart of Vancouver's hipster scene has also become one of the city's coolest and most welcoming neighborhoods in recent years. It's an inviting and easily accessible area to meet the locals and explore on your own away from the crowded city center. It's also brimming with indie stores, coffeeshops and intriguing eateries.

Getting There

🚇 Expo/Millennium Line from downtown to Main St–Science World station.

🚌 Number 3 from downtown runs along Main St; 99B-Line express stops at the Broadway and Main intersection.

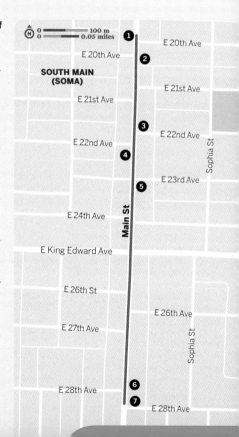

1 Browse the Racks at Neptoon Records

Vancouver's oldest independent record **store** (📞604-324-1229; www.neptoon. com; 3561 Main St; ⏲11am-6:30pm Mon-Sat, noon-5pm Sun; 🚌3) is a big lure for music fans. But it's not resting on its laurels; you'll find new and used vinyl and CDs plus serious help with finding that obscure Sigue Sigue Sputnik album you've been looking for.

2 Cool Clothing at Smoking Lily

Art-school cool rules at this mostly womenswear **boutique** (📞604-873-5459; www.smokinglily.com; 3634 Main St; ⏲11am-6pm Mon-Sat, noon-5pm Sun; 🚌3), with skirts and halter-tops whimsically accented with insects and anatomical heart motifs. Don't miss the accessories, including quirky purses beloved of Vancouver's pale and interesting set.

3 Vintage Togs at Front & Company

This popular triple-fronted **store** (📞604-879-8431; www.frontandcompany. ca; 3772 Main St; ⏲11am-6:30pm; 🚌3) contains trendy consignment clothing (perfect for vintage velvet smoking jackets), cool housewares and gift accessories, from manga figures to nihilist gum.

4 Early Dinner at the Fish Counter

A tasty fish and chip **cafe** (📞604-876-3474; www.thefishcounter.com; 3825 Main St; mains $10-22; ⏲10am-8pm; 🚌3) com-bining a fresh seafood counter and bustling fry operation. Order from the cashier in the middle, hit the stand-up inside table or sit-down benches outside and wait to be called. Locals love the juicy battered salmon.

5 Letter-writing at the Regional Assembly of Text

This digital-age **stationery store** (📞604-877-2247; www.assemblyoftext. com; 3934 Main St; ⏲11am-6pm Mon-Sat, noon-5pm Sun; 🚌3) lures ink-stained locals with its charming journals and pencil boxes. Don't miss the monthly **Letter Writing Club** where you can hammer erudite missives on vintage typewriters.

6 Late Opening at Red Cat Records

If you miss letter-writing night, hit the Friday or Saturday 8pm late opening at this **record shop** (📞604-708-9422; www.redcat.ca; 4332 Main St; ⏲11am-7pm Mon-Thu, to 8pm Fri & Sat, to 6pm Sun; 🚌3). Looking for the Red Cat? His name was Buddy and, although he's passed away, he's fondly remembered.

7 Nightcap at the Shameful Tiki Room

This windowless **cocktail bar** (www. shamefultikiroom.com; 4362 Main St; ⏲5pm-midnight Sun-Thu, to 1am Fri & Sat; 🚌3) evokes a Polynesian beach with its dusk lighting, tiki masks and straw ceiling. Dive into Zombies and a four-person Volcano Bowl (but don't forget to share).

Explore

Fairview & South Granville

Combining the boutiques and restaurants of well-to-do South Granville with Fairview's busy Broadway thoroughfare and cozy Cambie Village area, this Vancouver swath has something for everyone. It's a great area for meeting the locals where they live, shop and socialize. Green-thumbed visitors should also save time for some top-notch park and garden attractions in this part of the city.

The Sights in a Day

Start in **Queen Elizabeth Park** (pictured; p94) with some handsome panoramic views of Vancouver; expect your camera to work overtime if it's a clear day and you can also see the mountains beyond. After perusing the park's ornamental gardens, head inside to **Bloedel Conservatory** (p94), a climate-controlled rainforest with many brightly colored birds flitting about.

Dive into a tasty Mexican lunch at the ever-friendly **La Taqueria Pinche Taco Shop** (p94) (arrive offpeak to avoid the line-ups) then stroll uphill to **City Hall**. This handsome art deco landmark also has a photo-worthy statue of Captain George Vancouver outside.

Arrive before closing time to peruse the art, fashion and housewares boutiques on South Granville St. Save time for an end of-afternoon gin and tonic with the locals at **Marquis** (p97) then weave across the street (look both ways) for dinner at the excellent **Heirloom Vegetarian** (p96). Time for a nightcap? Don't miss beer (and a board game) at **Storm Crow Alehouse** (p97).

For a local's day in South Granville, see p90.

 Top Sights

VanDusen Botanical Garden (p88)

Local Life

South Granville Stroll (p90)

Best of Vancouver

Eating

Vij's (p95)

La Taqueria Pinche Taco Shop (p94)

Drinking

Storm Crow Alehouse (p97)

Outdoors

VanDusen Botanical Garden (p88)

Queen Elizabeth Park (p94)

Getting There

Train Cambie Village is sandwiched between Canada Line SkyTrain stations Broadway-City Hall and King Edward. The rest of Fairview radiates from the Broadway–City Hall station.

Bus Number 15 runs along Cambie St; 10 along South Granville. The two streets are linked by the 99B-Line and slower number 9.

Top Sights
VanDusen Botanical Garden

Vancouver's favorite manicured green space is a delightful confection of verdant walkways fringed by local and exotic flora. Just wandering around the mirror-calm lake is enough to slow your heart rate to tranquility levels – a useful reminder that there's more to the world than your cellphone screen. Don't throw it in the water, though; you'll need it to snap photos.

👁 Map p92, B8

📞 604-257-8335

www.vandusengarden.org

5251 Oak St

adult/child Apr-Sep $12.25/5.75

🕒 9am-8:30pm Jun-Aug

🚌 17

Plantlife

Opened in 1975, this 22-hectare green-thumbed wonderland is home to more than 250,000 plants representing some of the world's most distinct growing regions. You'll find trees, shrubs, flowers, succulents and more from across Canada, the Mediterranean, South Africa and the Himalayas, many of them identified with little plaques near their roots. There's almost always something in bloom here; if you're lucky, that might include the eye-popping **Rhododendron Walk** or neon-yellow, tunnel-like **Laburnum Walk**. Pick-up a self-guided tour sheet from the front desk for seasonal tips on what to see, or time your visit for a free guided tour.

Wildlife

It's not just humans that are lured by this sparkling stretch of nature; this is also a wildlife haven. Look out for turtles, herons and a variety of ducks in and around the main lake. You might also see owls, bats, raccoons or the occasional coyote in quiet corners. But birds are the main critters here. There's a downloadable checklist of feathered stars to look out for on VanDusen's website; highlights that lure camera lenses include eagles, hummingbirds and woodpeckers but there are dozens more.

Elizabethan Maze

Grown from more than 3000 pyramidal cedars, VanDusen's giggle-triggering traditional maze is the perfect spot to tire out your kids. Alternatively, just send them in there alone while you take a break outside. Now more than 25 years old, the maze has just the right combination of confusing dead-ends and gratifying solvability to give most visitors an entertaining diversion.

☑ Top Tips

▶ Quiz the docents. These wandering volunteers are a font of knowledge about what plants and wildlife to spot during your visit.

▶ VanDusen is also studded with garden artworks; see how many you can spot as you explore the walkways.

▶ The onsite **Garden Shop** is stuffed with excellent books and gifts for the botanically inclined.

▶ Visiting Vancouver in December? VanDusen's **Festival of Lights** is a local Christmas tradition with thousands of twinkling bulbs strung throughout the gardens.

✕ Take a Break

Head to VanDusen's **Truffles Cafe** (☏604-505-4961; www.trufflesfine foods.com; mains $5-9; ☺8:30am-8pm) for light lunches and fairtrade coffee. A patio table facing the garden is recommended.

Local Life
South Granville Stroll

Once the only independent-gallery district in the city (there are still more than a few to peruse here), South Granville is now better known as a UK-style outdoor shopping street that's well worth a stroll and a browse. There's plenty to consider buying here, plus more than a few places to stop for refreshments or a more substantial refueling.

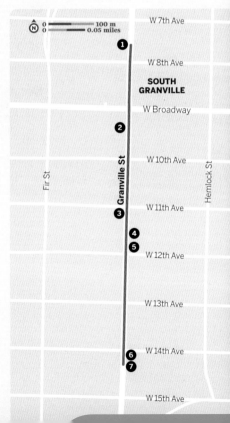

① Artwork Browsing at Ian Tan Gallery
For a chin-rubbing look at modern Canadian art, this **gallery** (p101) is worth visiting. Even if you don't go in, there are often some intriguing murals painted on the exterior wall alongside. Don't buy anything too large or you'll have to carry it on the uphill stretch accurately known as South Granville Rise.

2 Interior Design Ideas at Resoration Hardware

Pick up some inspiration for your dowdy, paint-peeled place back home at this highly popular, somewhat chichi **store** (p101). It's one of many similarly higher-end housewares shops on this slightly posh shopping street, indicating the proximity of the wealthy Shaughnessy neighborhood nearby.

3 Treat Stop at Purdy's Chocolates

This purple Vancouver-favorite chocolate **purveyor** (p101) at the corner of W 11th Ave is sure to entice you. Be sure to sample its Sweet Georgia Browns – pecans in caramel and chocolate. It is a local BC chain with stores located all around the city.

4 Matinee at the Stanley Theatre

This heritage **theater** (p99) hosts big musicals during the early summer months and contemporary productions during the rest of the year.

5 Cool Trinkets at Bacci's

With a brightly painted mural exterior (especially on the south side), this **store** (p99) is a Vancouver favorite that has designer women's clothing down one side and must-have housewares in a room on the other side.

6 Culinary Worship at Meinhardt Fine Foods

The packed aisles and shelves at this **deli** (p99) and food emporium are lined with international delicacies and gourmet treats.

7 Coffee at Bump n Grind

Grab a cup of joe and settle in at the big communal table of this Vancouver coffee chain's neighborhood **branch** (p97).

W 20th Ave
W 21st Ave
W 22nd Ave
W 23rd Ave

Manitoba St
W King Edward Ave

Peveril Ave

Hillcrest
Park

Dinmont Ave

15 ☆ Nat Bailey
Stadium

Midlothian Ave

Talismon St
Yukon St

Queen
Elizabeth
Park

1
2

Bloedel
Conservatory

For reviews see

◆	Top Sights	p88
◎	Sights	p94
✕	Eating	p94
▣	Drinking	p97
✦	Entertainment	p99
⌂	Shopping	p99

King
Edward
SkyTrain

Cambie St

Kersland Dr

W 26th Ave
W 27th Ave
W 28th Ave
W 29th Ave

W 33rd Ave

Heather St

W 37th Ave

Douglas
Park

W 22nd Ave
W 23rd Ave
W 24th Ave

Laurel S

Braemar
Park

CAMBIE

BC Children's
Hospital

Willow St

Oak St

Osler St

Selkirk St

Hudson St
W King Edward Ave

Balfour Ave
Laurier Ave

W 26th Ave
Nanton Ave
Devonshire Cr

Devonshire
Park

Connaught Dr

W 32nd Ave

W 33rd Ave

Oak St

VanDusen
Botanical Garden

◆

W 37th Ave

Granville St

5
6
7
8

E
D
C
B
A

Sights

Bloedel Conservatory

GARDENS

1 Map p92, D7

Cresting the hill in Queen Elizabeth Park, this balmy, triodetic-domed conservatory is an ideal rainy-day warm-up spot, as well as Vancouver's best-value attraction. For little more than the price of a latte, you'll find tropical trees and plants bristling with hundreds of free-flying, bright-plumaged birds. Look for the resident parrots as well as rainbow-hued Gouldian finches, shimmering African superb starlings and maybe a sparkling Lady Amherst pheasant, snaking through the undergrowth. The attendants might even let you feed the smaller birds from a bowl. (604-257-8584; www.vandusengarden. org; Queen Elizabeth Park, 4600 Cambie St; adult/child $6.75/3.25; 9am-8pm Mon-Fri, 10am-8pm Sat & Sun May-Aug, 10am-5pm daily Sep-Apr; P; 15)

Queen Elizabeth Park

PARK

2 Map p92, D7

The city's highest point – it's 167m above sea level and has panoramic views of the mountain-framed downtown skyscrapers – this 52-hectare park claims to house specimens of every tree native to Canada. Sports fields, manicured lawns and two formal gardens keep the locals happy, and you'll likely also see wide-eyed couples posing for their wedding photos. (www.vancouverparks.ca; entrance cnr W 33rd Ave & Cambie St; P; 15)

Eating

La Taquería Pinche Taco Shop

MEXICAN $

3 Map p92, D2

This popular taco spot expanded from its tiny Hastings St location (which is still there) with this larger storefront. It's just as crowded but luckily many of the visitors are going the take-out route. Nab a brightly painted table, then order at the counter from a dozen or so meat or veggie soft tacos (take your pick or ask for a selection). (604-558-2549; www.lataqueria.ca; 2549 Cambie St, Fairview; 4 tacos $8.50-10.50; 11am-8:30pm Mon-Sat, noon-6pm Sun; ; SBroadway-City Hall)

Beaucoup Bakery & Cafe

CAFE $

4 Map p92, A2

Vancouverites used to content themselves with humdrum croissants and lame French pastries that would be laughed off the counter in Paris – until this amazing bakery opened. Now, it's the pilgrimage spot of choice for eye-rollingly amazing treats from cinnamon scrolls to completely irresistible peanut-butter-sandwich cookies. And as for the croissants, they're the best in the city: shatteringly crisp with chewy-soft interiors. (604-732-4222; www.beaucoupbakery.com; 2150 Fir St, South Granville; cakes & sandwiches under $10; 7am-5pm Mon-Fri, 8am-5pm Sat & Sun; 4)

STEPHEN CHUNG/SHUTTERSTOCK ©

Parrot at Bloedel Conservatory

Vij's
INDIAN $$$

5 Map p92, D4

A sparkling (and far larger) new location for Canada's favorite East Indian chef delivers a warmly sumptuous lounge coupled with a cavernous dining area and cool rooftop patio. The menu, a high-water mark of contemporary Indian cuisine, fuses BC ingredients, global flourishes and classic ethnic flavors to produce many inventive dishes. Results range from signature 'lamb popsicles' to flavorful meals such as sablefish in yogurt-tomato broth. (☏604-736-6664; www.vijs restaurant.ca; 3106 Cambie St, Cambie Village; mains $19-27; ⊗5:30-10pm; ✎; ☐15)

Rain or Shine
ICE CREAM $

6 Map p92, D4

Under the gaze of a cone-crowned purple cow on the wall, you may have to queue at this finger-licking ice-cream emporium. But that will give you time to mull the flavors, which range from – on our visit – crushed mint to blueberry balsamic. All are made on site and served in cups or cones, although perhaps staff will shovel it straight into your mouth if you ask nicely. (☏604-876-9986; www. rainorshineicecream.com; 3382 Cambie St, Cambie Village; ⊗noon-10pm; ☝; ☐15)

Local Life

Cambie Village Dining

An ever-inviting neighborhood eatery, **Pronto** (Map p92, D4; ☏604-722-9331; www.prontocaffe.ca; 3473 Cambie St, Cambie Village; mains $14-22; ⊙11:30am-9pm Sun, Tue & Wed, to 10pm Thu-Sat; ☒15) is a charming Cambie Village trattoria combining woodsy candlelit booths, perfectly prepared housemade pasta and the kind of warm service few restaurants manage to provide. Drop by for a lunchtime porchetta sandwich, or come for dinner, when the intimate, wood-floored space feels deliciously relaxed. Check the blackboard specials or head straight for the gnocchi with pesto and pancetta.

Heirloom Vegetarian VEGETARIAN $$

7 Map p92, A3

With a white-walled cafeteria-meets-rustic artisan look (hence the farm implements on the wall), this is one of Vancouver's tastiest vegetarian options, serving mostly BC and organic seasonal ingredients fused with international influences. Locals love the shiny-bunned Royale burger with its addictive yam fries accompaniment. There's also a page of vegan options on the menu; we recommend the nicely spiced pineapple coconut curry. (☏604-733-2231; www.heirloomrestaurant. ca; 1509 W 12th Ave, South Granville; mains $14-20; ⊙9am-10pm; ☑; ☒10)

Paul's Omelettery BREAKFAST $

8 Map p92, A2

You'll be jostling for space with chatty moms at this unassuming breakfast and lunch joint near the south side of Granville Bridge. But this cozy, super-friendly place is superior to most bacon-and-eggs spots. The menu is grounded on signature omelets but it also does great eggs Benedict and there are housemade burgers and sandwiches at lunch. (☏604-737-2857; www.paulsomelettery.com; 2211 Granville St, South Granville; mains $8-14; ⊙7am-3pm; ☑♟; ☒10)

Salmon n' Bannock WEST COAST $$

9 Map p92, B2

Vancouver's only First Nations restaurant is a delightful art-lined little bistro on an unassuming strip of Broadway shops. It's worth the bus trip for fresh-made aboriginal-influenced dishes made with local ingredients. If lunching, try the signature (and juicy) salmon 'n' bannock burger, made with a traditional flatbread introduced by Scottish settlers which is now a staple of First Nations BC dining. (☏604-568-8971; www.salmon andbannock.net; 1128 W Broadway, Fairview; mains $14-24; ⊙11:30am-3pm & 5-9pm Mon-Thu, to 10pm Fri, 5-10pm Sat; ☒9)

Drinking

Elysian Coffee COFFEE

10 Map p92, D2

Just to show that not all the hipsters hang out on Main St, this neighborhood joint lures every skinny-jeaned local in its vicinity. They come for the excellent coffee (it's not just about looking cool here) plus a small array of baked treats and some very tempting home coffee-making paraphernalia. Take a seat at the front window and watch Broadway bustle past. (www.elysiancoffee.com; 590 W Broadway, Fairview; ⊗7am-7pm; ☎; ⊕9)

Bump n Grind COFFEE

11 Map p92, A3

The South Granville branch of this two-outlet local coffeehouse chain has a great long table at the back where you can settle down with a java and peruse the tiny wall-mounted library of handmade zines. Alternatively, press your face against the glass cabinet of bakery treats at the front and try to levitate a curried butternut-squash muffin into your mouth. (☎604-558-4743; www.bumpngrindcafe.com; 3010 Granville St, South Granville; ⊗7am-7pm Mon-Fri, 8am-7pm Sat & Sun; ☎; ⊕10)

Marquis BAR

12 Map p92, A3

Don't blink or you'll miss the entrance to this cozy hidden nook that's popular with locals meeting to start their night out or dropping by for a nightcap

before bed. Find a perch at the high tables facing the bar and tuck into a menu of classic martinis and flirty cocktails (plus some nice bottled beer imports). (☎604-568-0670; www.themarquis.ca; 2666 Granville St, South Granville; ⊗4pm-2am Mon-Sat, to midnight Sun; ⊕10)

Biercraft Bistro BEER HALL

13 Map p92, D4

With a wood-lined interior plus two popular street-side patios, this beer-forward resto-bar is a great spot for ale aficionados. Dive into the astonishing array of Belgian tipples and compare them to some choice microbrews from BC and the US.

 Local Life

Drinking with the Romulans

The larger sibling of Commercial Dr's excellent nerd bar, **Storm Crow Alehouse** (Map p92, A2; ☎604-428-9670; www.stormcrowalehouse.com; 1619 W Broadway, South Granville; ⊗11am-1am Mon-Thu, 11am-2am Fri, 9am-2am Sat, 9am-1am Sun; ⊕9) welcomes everyone from the Borg to beardy *Lord of the Rings* dwarfs. They come to peruse the memorabilia-studded walls (think Millennium Falcon models and a Tardis washroom door), play the board games and dive into apposite refreshments including Romulan Ale and Pangalactic Gargleblasters. Hungry? Miss the chunky chickpea fries at your peril.

Understand
Animal Watch

Common Critters

Vancouver's urban green spaces are home to a surprising array of wildlife. During your visit, you'll find black squirrels everywhere, but don't be surprised to also spot raccoons. Common in several parks, they are often bold enough to hang out on porches and root through garbage bins. Skunks are almost as common, but the only time you'll likely see them is after an unfortunate roadkill incident (a regular occurrence around area parks). But while squirrels, raccoons and skunks are regarded as urban nuisances, some animals in the city are much larger.

Bigger Critters

Every spring, several Vancouver neighborhoods post notices of coyote spottings (there are an estimated 3000 living in and around the city). This is the time of year when the wolflike wild dogs build dens and raise pups, often in remote corners of city parks – and they become more protective of their territory in the process. Vancouverites are warned to keep pets inside when coyotes are spotted in their neighborhoods, and report any sightings to authorities. Most locals will tell you they've rarely seen a coyotes– the animals are mostly very adept at avoiding humans.

Birdlife

At the other end of the scale, Vancouver is a great city for bird spotters. In Queen Elizabeth Park, keep your eyes peeled for bald eagles whirling overhead. On Granville Island, glance up under Granville Bridge and you'll find cormorants treating the girders like cliffside roosts. And if you're anywhere near a pond, you might see coots, wood ducks and statue-still herons alongside the ubiquitous Canada Geese.

On streets around the city, also look out for northern flicker woodpeckers (known for their red cheeks and black-spotted plumage) plus finches, chickadees and Steller's jays, BC's provincial bird. You might even spot what many regard as an unlikely year-round local here: the delightful little Anna's hummingbird. In spring and summer, it's joined by the migrating rufous hummingbird. They're the reason you'll spot sugar-water feeders on balconies across the city.

Save time for food; the slightly pricey gastropub menu here ranges from steak *frites* to bowls of locally sourced mussels in several brothy iterations. (📞604-874-6900; www.biercraft.com; 3305 Cambie St, Cambie Village; ⏰11:30am-midnight Mon-Thu, 11:30am-1am Fri, 10am-1am Sat, 10am-midnight Sun; 🚌15)

Entertainment

Stanley Theatre THEATER

14 ⭐ Map p92, A3

Popular musicals dominate early summer (usually the last show of the season) at this heritage theater, but the rest of the year sees new works and adaptations of contemporary hits from around the world. Officially called the Stanley Industrial Alliance Stage (a moniker that not a single Vancouverite uses), the Stanley is part of the Arts Club Theatre Company, Vancouver's biggest. (📞604-687-1644; www.artsclub.com; 2750 Granville St, South Granville; tickets from $29; ⏰Sep-Jun; 🚌10)

Vancouver Canadians BASEBALL

15 ⭐ Map p92, E7

Minor-league affiliates of the Toronto Blue Jays, the Canadians play at the charmingly old-school Nat Bailey Stadium. It's known as 'the prettiest ballpark in the world' thanks to its mountain backdrop. Afternoon games – called 'nooners' – are perfect for a nostalgic bask in the sun. Hot dogs and beer rule the menu, but there's also sushi and fruit – this is Vancouver, after all. (📞604-872-5232; www.canadiansbaseball.com; Nat Bailey Stadium, 4601 Ontario St; tickets $11-25; ⏰Jun-Sep; 🚌33, Ⓢ King Edward)

Shopping

Bacci's HOMEWARES, CLOTHING

16 Map p92, A3

Combining designer women's clothing on one side with a room full of perfectly curated trinkets piled high on antique wooden tables on the other, Bacci's is a dangerous place to browse. Before you know it, you'll have an armful of chunky luxury soaps, embroidered cushions and picture-perfect coffee mugs to fit in your suitcase. (📞604-733-4933; www.baccis.ca; 2788 Granville St, South Granville; ⏰9:45am-5:45pm Mon-Sat; 🚌10)

Meinhardt Fine Foods FOOD

17 Map p92, A3

The culinary equivalent of a sex shop for food fans, this swanky deli and grocery emporium's narrow aisles are lined with international condiments, luxury canned goods and the kind of tempting treats that everyone should try at least once. Drop by for Christmas goodies or build your perfect picnic from the tempting bread, cheese and cold-cuts selections. (📞604-732-4405; www.meinhardt.com; 3002 Granville St, South Granville; ⏰8am-9pm Mon-Sat, 9am-8pm Sun; 🚌10)

Shop Cocoon

CLOTHING

18 🔒 Map p92, D4

A narrow, inviting little boutique showcasing a carefully chosen array of North American and international designer women's clothing, from natty summer dresses to flirty tops and cute jeans. A Cambie Village favorite, it also stocks extras such as locally made jewelry and handmade soap, artfully presented on antique bookcases. Ask the famously solicitous staff for tips on other stores to check out around the city. (☎778-232-8532; www.shopcocoon.com; 3345 Cambie St, Cambie Village; ⏱11am-7pm Tue-Sat, 11am-6pm Sun; 🚌15)

Walrus

HOMEWARES

19 🔒 Map p92, D4

A small but perfectly curated store teeming with superbly designed homewares and accessories that are almost impossible to resist. Form meets function in everything on the shelves here, including excellent travel clocks, mod coffee pots with a knowing nod to the 1970s and must-have Mondaine watches for all you style mavens. Your credit card will soon be sweating. (☎604-874-9770; www.walrushome.com; 3408 Cambie St, Cambie Village; ⏱10am-7pm Mon-Fri, 10am-5pm Sat, noon-5pm Sun; 🚌15)

Understand
City Hall Story

The Great Depression caused major belt-tightening among the regular folks of 1930s Vancouver. But, despite the economic malaise, mayor Gerry McGeer spared no expense when building a new **City Hall** (Map p92, D3; www.vancouver.ca; 453 W 12th Ave, Fairview; admission free; ⏱8:30am-5pm Mon-Fri; Ⓢ Broadway–City Hall) in 1936. Defending the grand art-deco edifice he planned as a make-work project for the idled construction industry, the $1 million project (a very large sum for the time) was completed in just 12 months.

But while McGeer wasn't always a friend to the working classes. Believing that radicalism was taking hold among out-of-work Vancouverites, he ordered police to crack down on protests whenever they emerged. When hundreds gathered to call for jobs in East Vancouver's Victory Sq, McGeer turned up to read them the riot act. A few weeks later, police and hundreds of protesters fought a three-hour street battle with rocks, clubs and tear gas. Rumors at the time said the police were preparing to use machine guns against the crowd when it began to disperse. The infamous incident was later named the Battle of Ballantyne Pier.

Ian Tan Gallery
ARTS & CRAFTS

20 Map p92, A2

While some private galleries can seem intimidating (perhaps purposely), this popular stop on the city's one-time gallery row is the opposite. It recently relocated from its original premises across the street. Step inside for bold, often bright contemporary works. Canadian artists are the main focus here. (604-738-1077; www.iantangallery.com; 2321 Granville St, South Granville; 10am-6pm Mon-Sat; 10)

Purdy's Chocolates
FOOD

21 Map p92, A3

Like a beacon to the weary, this purple-painted chocolate store stands at the corner of Granville and W 11th Ave. It's a homegrown BC business with outlets dotted like candy sprinkles across the city, and it's hard not to pick up a few treats: go for chocolate hedgehogs, mint meltie bars or Sweet Georgia Browns – pecans in caramel and chocolate. (604-732-7003; 2705 Granville St, South Granville; 10am-6pm Mon-Sat, noon-5pm Sun; 10)

Restoration Hardware
HOMEWARES

22 Map p92, A2

Filled with furnishings and interior flourishes that you wish you had in

DOUGLAS WILLIAMS/AGEFOTOSTOCK ©

Stanley Theatre (p99)

your house, this upmarket favorite also carries occasional kitsch-tastic reproduction toys and old-school gadgets, especially at Christmastime. Even if you don't buy anything, it's a great place to poke around and get some ideas for your summer house in the south of France. (604-731-3918; www.restorationhardware.com; 2555 Granville St, South Granville; 10am-7pm Mon-Sat, 11am-6pm Sun; 10)

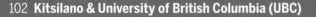

Explore

Kitsilano & University of British Columbia (UBC)

Occupying the forest-fringed peninsula to the south of downtown, Vancouver's West Side includes two major highlights: Kitsilano, with its heritage homes, beaches and 4th Ave shopping and dining district; and, on the tip of the peninsula, the University of British Columbia (UBC; pictured), a verdant campus with enough museums, galleries, attractions and dining options for a great day out.

The Sights in a Day

☼ Grab coffee with the students at UBC before checking out the taxidermied critter collection at the **Beaty Biodiversity Museum** (p110). There's a great little gift shop here if you're shopping for nature-huggers back home. Commune with the natural world yourself at the verdant **UBC Botanical Garden** (p110), especially if the annual Apple Fest is in full swing.

☼ If the ocean is suddenly calling you like a siren song, make for **Kitsilano Beach** (p113) and breathe in some stirring views of the West Coast shoreline. Bracing weather? Head over to **Silk Road Tea** (p116) for some warming leaf-based elixirs or snag a late lunch at **Fable** (p113), both located on shop-and-restaurant-lined 4th Ave.

☾ Head over to Vanier Park before closing time at the **Museum of Vancouver** (p110) and immerse yourself in the city's colorful past. You can grab drinks and dinner at **Corduroy** (p114) just outside the park but, if it's summertime, make sure you're back for the evening Shakespeare show at **Bard on the Beach** (p116), an annual Vancouver tradition.

For a local's day in UBC, see p106.

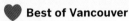 **Top Sights**

Museum of Anthropology (p104)

◯ **Local Life**

UBC Campus & Gardens Walk (p106)

♥ **Best of Vancouver**

Eating
Mr Red Cafe (p112)

Fable (p113)

Outdoors
UBC Botanical Garden (p110)

Pacific Spirit Regional Park (p110)

Shopping
Stepback (p116)

Getting There

🚌 **Bus** Services 4 and 9 run through Kitsilano, eventually reaching UBC. The 99B-Line express runs on Broadway to UBC.

🚈 **Train** Take the Canada Line to Broadway-City Hall, then hop bus 9 or 99B-Line along Broadway to UBC.

Top Sights
Museum of Anthropology

Vancouver's best museum is the main reason many visitors come to the University of British Columbia campus. The MOA is home to one of Canada's finest and most important collections of northwest coast aboriginal art and artifacts. But that's just the start; the ambitious collection here goes way beyond local anthropological treasures, illuminating diverse cultures from around the world.

◉ Map p108, A3

☏ 604-822-5087

www.moa.ubc.ca

6393 NW Marine Dr

adult/child $18/16

🕑 10am-5pm Wed-Sun, to 9pm Thu

🚍 99B-Line

MOA 101

The highlight of the Arthur Erickson–designed museum, the grand **Great Hall** is a forest of towering totem poles plus carved ceremonial figures and exhibits set against a giant floor-to-ceiling window. Many of the ornate carvings are vibrantly colored: look out for some smiling masks as well as a life-sized rowing boat containing two figures that look ready to head straight out to sea. This is also where the **free tours** depart several times a day.

Getting Lost

If you miss the tour or just want to go at your own pace, this is also a good museum in which to get lost. And, despite its reputation for only showcasing Aboriginal culture, there is much more to be seen than you'd imagine. The renovation enabled more of the university's immense collection to be displayed in the jam-packed **Multiversity Galleries**. There are more than 10,000 fascinating and often eye-popping ethnographic artifacts from around the world, squeezed into display cabinets. You'll find everything from Kenyan snuff bottles to Navajo blankets from the US.

Value-added Extras

Aside from the regular permanent galleries, there are some diverse temporary exhibitions during the year. Do not leave before you've checked these out. Recent visiting shows have included Buddhist art, Peruvian silverware and First Nations treasures from across BC and beyond. Check the MOA's website calendar before you arrive and you'll also find lectures, movies and presentations, as well as occasional live music performances, which are often staged in the grand Great Hall. Some shows and presentations are included with your admission.

☑ Top Tips

▶ Admission is cut to $10 from 5pm to 9pm every Thursday.

▶ There are free tours, included with entry, on most days. Check at the front desk for times.

▶ There are several other attractions on campus. Add galleries, gardens and other museums for a full UBC day out.

✕ Take a Break

The MOA is a short walk from the excellent Koerner's Pub (p114), where you can drink and dine with the students.

Local Life
UBC Campus & Gardens Walk

Vancouverites are fully aware that the region's biggest university campus has more than enough attractions for a full day out. This walk introduces you to some of the lesser-known lures here, including cultural sites and delightful gardens. Keep your eyes peeled – and your camera ready – for glimpses of the dramatic shoreline location and the many public artworks dotting the campus.

1 **Coffee at the Nest**

Not far from the bus loop where most visitors arrive on campus, the sparkling new Student Union Building – aka the **Nest** – is twice as big as the dark old red-brick original next door. It's a good spot to fuel up, meet the student populace and browse a copy of campus newspaper *The Ubyssey*.

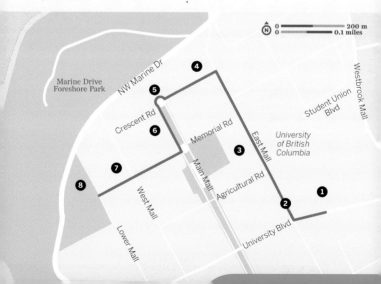

2 East Mall Amble

The adjoining East Mall is your introduction to UBC's vast menu of public artworks. Look for the *Victory Through Honour* totem pole outside **Brock Hall**, created by the region's Musqueam First Nation plus *Untitled (Symbols for Education)*, a huge modernist mural from the 1950s.

3 Secret Museum

Descend to the basement of the cavernous **UBC library.** You'll find a small, well-hidden museum that only some locals know about. Housing the Chung Collection, it includes evocative photos illuminating Vancouver's early Chinese residents plus nostalgic posters from the golden age of Canadian rail travel.

4 Check out the Chan Centre

A dramatic elliptical theater rising into the sky, this state-of-the-art 1997-opened concert venue is popular with locals on this side of the city. There are often classical performances on stage, including shows by the celebrated Vancouver Symphony Orchestra. Check the calendar before you arrive, to see what's coming up.

5 Sniff out the Rose Garden

The best spot on campus for dramatic scenic photos is on the promontory just above thie fragrant, meticulously landscaped rose garden. Take your photos first; the garden with shimmering mountain backdrop is a signature UBC view. Then poke around the ornamental garden, planted with hundreds of rose varieties.

6 Peruse the Morris and Helen Belkin Gallery

This inviting **gallery** (p112) features modern and some provocative works. Inside, you can expect temporary exhibitions plus a permanent collection of avant-garde art.

7 Pit Stop outside the UBC Asian Centre

The campus has many different schools and research areas. And despite the sometimes labyrinthine layout, you'll come across more than a few on your wander. The UBC Asian Centre has been here for years but check out the rock garden alongside; its boulders are inscribed with Confucian philosophies.

8 Explore the Nitobe Memorial Garden

Continue on and immerse yourself in this calming Japanese **oasis** (p112) featuring beautiful bridges and a koi pond. It's named after Dr Inazo Nitobe, the scholar appearing on Japan's ¥5000 note.

A B C D

1

N
0 ——————— 1 km
0 ——————— 0.5 miles

Burrard Inlet

Spanish Banks
Beach Park

NW Marine Dr

2

Marine Drive
Foreshore
Park

Acadia Rd

Kingston Rd

*Pacific Spirit
Regional Park*

Blanca St

Tolmie St

Belmont Ave

Chancellor Blvd

W 2nd Ave

**Museum of
Anthropology**

NW Marine Dr

Knox Rd

Allison Rd

Western Pkwy

W 3rd Ave

W 4th Ave

Morris and
Helen Belkin
Gallery

14 7

Main Mall

University Blvd

W 6th Ave

W 8th Ave

West Point
Grey Park

3

6

Nitobe
Memorial
Garden

*University
of British
Columbia*

4

Beaty
Biodiversity
Museum

East Mall

Westbrook Mall

*University
Golf Club*

W 10th Ave

W 12th Ave

W 14th Ave

Sasamat St

Trimble St

Discovery St

3

W 16th Ave

West Mall

Pacific Spirit
Regional Park

UBC
Botanical
Garden

4

2

Thunderbird
Stadium

W 16th Ave

Pacific Spirit
Regional Park

Point
NoPoint

SW Marine Dr

Old Marine Dr

Imperial Rd

*Strait of
Georgia*

DUNBAR

5

Marine Drive
Foreshore Park

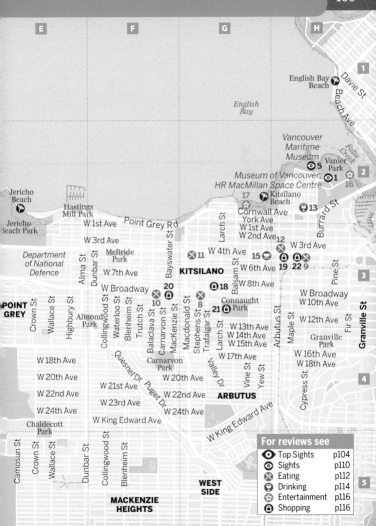

E F G H

1

English Bay
Beach

Davie St

Beach Ave

English
Bay

Vancouver
Maritime
Museum
⊙ 5 Vanier
Park

2

Museum of Vancouver;
HR MacMillan Space Centre
⊙ 1

16

False Creek

Jericho
Beach

Hastings
Mill Park

17 ✪ Kitsilano
Beach

Cornwall Ave
York Ave

13

Jericho
Beach Park

Point Grey Rd

W 1st Ave

Larch St

W 1st Ave
W 2nd Ave

Burrard St

W 3rd Ave

Department
of National
Defence

Alma St

Dunbar St

McBride
Park

Bayswater St

✕ 11 W 4th Ave

12

W 3rd Ave

15 ⊙ 19 ⊕ ⊕ 9
22

KITSILANO

Balsam St

W 6th Ave

3

W 7th Ave

W Broadway

20 ✕

Broadway

Pine St

W Broadway
W 10th Ave

POINT
GREY

Crown St

Wallace St

Highbury St

Collingwood St

Waterloo St

Blenheim St

Trutch St

10
⊕

W 8th Ave

18 ⊕

Macdonald St

Stephens St

8 ✕ Connaught
Park
21 ⊕

Larch St

Arbutus St

Maple St

W 12th Ave

Fir St

Granville
Park

Granville St

Almond
Park

Balaclava St

Carnarvon St

Mackenzie St

Trafalgar St

W 13th Ave
W 14th Ave
W 15th Ave

Vine St

Yew St

W 16th Ave
W 18th Ave

Cypress St

4

W 18th Ave

W 20th Ave

W 22nd Ave

W 24th Ave

Carnarvon
Park

Quesnel Dr

Puget Dr

W 21st Ave

W 23rd Ave

W King Edward Ave

W 20th Ave

W 22nd Ave

W 24th Ave

Valley Dr

ARBUTUS

W King Edward Ave

Chaldecott
Park

Camosun St

Crown St

Wallace St

Dunbar St

Collingwood St

Blenheim St

WEST
SIDE

5

MACKENZIE
HEIGHTS

Sights

Museum of Vancouver   MUSEUM

1 Map p108, H2

The MOV has hugely improved in recent years, with cool temporary exhibitions and evening events aimed at culturally minded adults. It hasn't changed everything, though. There are still superbly evocative displays on local 1950s pop culture and 1960s hippie counterculture – a reminder that 'Kits' was once the grass-smoking center of Vancouver's flower-power movement – plus a shimmering gallery of vintage neon signs from around the city. (MOV; ☎604-736-4431; www.museumofvancouver.ca; 1100 Chestnut St; adult/child $15/5; ⏰10am-5pm, to 8pm Thu; 🅿♿; 🚍22)

UBC Botanical Garden   GARDENS

2 Map p108, A4

You'll find a giant collection of rhododendrons, a fascinating apothecary plot and a winter green space of off-season bloomers in this 28-hectare complex of themed gardens. Save time for the attraction's **Greenheart Tree-Walk** (☎604-822-4208; ⏰10am-4:30pm daily, to 7:30pm Thu Apr-Oct; 🅿♿), which lifts visitors 17m above the forest floor on a 308m guided ecotour. A combined botanical garden and walkway ticket costs $20. (www.botanicalgarden. ubc.ca; 6804 SW Marine Dr; adult/child $9/5; ⏰9:30am-4:30pm, to 8pm Thu mid-Mar–Oct, 9:30am-4pm Nov–mid-Mar; 🚍99 B-Line, then C20)

Pacific Spirit Regional Park   PARK

3 Map p108, C4

This stunning 763-hectare park stretches from Burrard Inlet to the North Arm of the Fraser River, a green buffer zone between the UBC campus and the city. A smashing spot to explore with 70km of walking, jogging and cycling trails, it includes **Camosun Bog wetland** (accessed by a boardwalk at 19th Ave and Camosun St), a bird and plant haven. (www. pacificspiritparksociety.org; cnr Blanca St & W 16th Ave; 🅿; 🚍99 B-Line)

Beaty Biodiversity Museum   MUSEUM

4 Map p108, A3

UBC's newest museum is also its most family-friendly. It showcases two million natural history specimens that have never before been available for public viewing: the museum features fossil, fish and herbarium displays. The highlight is the 25m blue whale skeleton, artfully displayed in the museum's two-story main entrance, plus the first display case, which is crammed with tooth-and-claw taxidermy. Check the schedule for free tours and kids' activities. (☎604-827-4955; www.beatymuseum.ubc.ca; 2212 Main Mall; adult/child $12/10; ⏰10am-5pm Tue-Sun; ♿; 🚍99B-Line)

DOUGLAS LANDER/AGEFOTOSTOCK ©

Beaty Biodiversity Museum

HR MacMillan Space Centre

MUSEUM

Popular with schoolkids – expect to have to elbow them out of the way to push the flashing buttons – this slightly dated science center at the Museum of Vancouver (see 1 ◉ Map p108, H2) illuminates the world of space. There's plenty of fun to be had battling aliens, designing spacecraft or strapping yourself in for a simulator ride to Mars, as well as with movie presentations on all manner of spacey themes. (☏604-738-7827; www.spacecentre.ca; 1100 Chestnut St; adult/child $18/13; ⊗10am-5pm Jul-Aug, 10am-3pm Mon-Fri, 10am-5pm Sat & noon-5pm Sun Sep-Jun; P♿; ☒22)

Vancouver Maritime Museum

MUSEUM

5 ◉ Map p108, H2

Combining dozens of intricate models, detailed re-created ship sections and some historic boats, the prize exhibit in this waterfront A-frame museum is the *St Roch*, a 1928 Royal Canadian Mounted Police Arctic patrol vessel that was the first to navigate the legendary Northwest Passage in both directions. On a budget? Thursday entry (after 5pm) is by donation. (www.vancouvermaritimemuseum. com; 1905 Ogden Ave; adult/child $11/8.50; ⊗10am-5pm, to 8pm Thu, reduced hours off-season; P; ☒22)

Top Tip

Save Your Dosh

The **Vanier Park Explore Pass** costs adult/child $36/30 and covers entry to the Museum of Vancouver, Vancouver Maritime Museum and HR MacMillan Space Centre. It's available at each of the three attractions and can save you around $10 on individual adult entry. You can also save with the **UBC Museums and Gardens Pass**. It costs adult/child $33/28 and includes entry to the Museum of Anthropology, Botanical Garden, Nitobe Memorial Garden and Beatty Biodiversity Museum. Available at any of these attractions, it also includes discounts for the Greenheart TreeWalk, plus deals on campus parking, dining and shopping.

Nitobe Memorial Garden GARDENS

 6 Map p108, A3

Exemplifying Japanese horticultural philosophies, this is a tranquil oasis of peaceful pathways, small traditional bridges and a large, moss-banked pond filled with plump koi carp. It's named after Dr Inazo Nitobe, a scholar whose mug appears on Japan's ¥5000 bill. Consider a springtime visit for the florid cherry-blossom displays. (www.nitobe.org; 1895 Lower Mall; adult/child $7/4; ⏰11am-4:30pm, to 8pm Thu mid-Mar–Oct, 10am-2pm Mon-Fri Nov–mid-Mar; 🚍99 B-Line, then C20)

Morris and Helen Belkin Gallery GALLERY

 7 Map p108, A3

This great little gallery specializes in contemporary and often quite challenging pieces – which explains the billboard-style depiction of an Iraqi city outside, complete with the caption 'Because there was and there wasn't a city of Baghdad.' Inside, you can expect a revolving roster of traveling shows plus chin-stroking exhibits from a permanent collection of Canadian avant-garde works. (📞604-822-2759; www.belkin.ubc.ca; 1825 Main Mall; admission free; ⏰10am-5pm Tue-Fri, noon-5pm Sat & Sun; 🚍99 B-Line)

Eating

Mr Red Cafe VIETNAMESE $

 8 Map p108, G3

Serves authentic northern Vietnamese homestyle dishes that look and taste like there's a lovely old lady making them out back. Reservations are not accepted; dine off-peak to avoid waiting for the handful of tables, then dive into shareable gems such as pork baguette sandwiches, *cha ca han oi* (spicy grilled fish) and the ravishing pyramidical rice dumpling, stuffed with pork and a boiled quail's egg. (📞604-559-6878; 2680 W Broadway; mains $6-14; ⏰11am-9pm; 🍴; 🚍9)

Fable

CANADIAN **$$**

9 Map p108, H3

One of Vancouver's favorite farm-to-table restaurants is a lovely rustic-chic room of exposed brick, wood beams and prominently displayed red rooster logos. But looks are just part of the appeal. Expect perfectly prepared bistro dishes showcasing local seasonal ingredients such as duck, lamb and halibut. It's great gourmet comfort food with little pretension – hence the packed room most nights. Reservations recommended. (📞604-732-1322; www.fablekitchen.ca; 1944 W 4th Ave; mains $19-31; ⏱11:30am-2pm Mon-Fri, 5:30-10pm Mon-Sat, brunch 10:30am-2pm Sat & Sun; 🚌4)

Maenam

THAI **$$**

Situated near Fable (see 9 Map p108, H3) Vancouver's best Thai restaurant is a contemporary reinvention of the concept, with subtle, complex influences flavoring the menu in a warm, wood-floored room with an inviting ambiance. You can start with the familiar (although even the pad Thai here is eye-poppingly different), but save room for something new, such as the utterly delicious black-pepper venison stir-fry. (📞604-730-5579; www.maenam.ca; 1938 W 4th Ave; mains $16-22; ⏱noon-2pm Tue-Sat, 5-10pm daily; 🖊; 🚌4)

Cartems Donuterie

BAKERY

10 Map p108, F3

The newest of a three-outlet gourmet doughnut mini-chain (the others are on Main St and downtown), this austere-looking L-shaped spot is all about indulging in that most vital of food groups: the treat. Snag a seat at the communal table and sink your choppers into salted caramel, Earl Grey or Canadian whiskey bacon varieties – or all three. Local-made Earnest Ice Cream is also served. (www.cartems.com; 3040 W Broadway; baked goods $3-4; ⏱8am-10pm Mon-Fri, 9am-10pm Sat, to 8pm Sun; 🚌9)

Naam

VEGETARIAN **$$**

11 Map p108, G3

An evocative relic of Kitsilano's hippie past, this vegetarian restaurant has the feel of a comfy farmhouse. It's not unusual to have to wait for a table at peak times, but it's worth it for the huge menu of hearty stir-fries, nightly curry specials, bulging quesadillas and ever-popular fries with miso gravy. It's the kind of veggie spot where carnivores

---

Local Life

Summer Hangouts

On languid summer days, everyone in Vancouver seems to be soaking up the rays at **Kitsilano Beach** (cnr Cornwall Ave & Arbutus St; 🚌22). Arrive early to find a good spot. Too crowded? There are several additional beaches along the West Side shoreline here, including Jericho Beach, Spanish Banks and – on the UBC campus – the clothing optional Wreck Beach.

delightedly dine. (604-738-7151; www.thenaam.com; 2724 W 4th Ave; mains $9-16; 24hr; 4)

Sophie's Cosmic Café

DINER $$

12 Map p108, H3

Slide between the oversized knife and fork flanking the entrance and step into one of Vancouver's favorite retro-look diners, with a cornucopia of kitsch lining the walls. Burgers and big-ass milkshakes dominate the menu, but breakfast is the best reason to come. Expect weekend queues as you await your appointment with a heaping plate of eggs and lamb mergeuz sausage. (604-732-6810; www.sophiescosmiccafe.com; 2095 West 4th Ave; mains $11-16; 8am-2:30pm Mon, 8am-8pm Tue-Sun; 4)

Drinking

Corduroy

BAR

13 Map p108, H2

Handily located near the first bus stop after the Burrard Bridge (coming from downtown), this tiny spot is arguably Kitsilano's best haunt. Slide onto a bench seat and peruse the oddball artworks – junk-shop pictures and carved masks – then order a house beer from the shingle-covered bar: if you're lucky, it'll be served in a boot-shaped glass. (604-733-0162; www.corduroyrestaurant.com; 1943 Cornwall Ave; 4pm-2am Mon-Sat, 4pm-midnight Sun; 22)

Koerner's Pub

PUB

14 Map p108, A3

UBC's best pub welcomes you with its communal tables, tree-fringed garden and clientele of nerdy professors and hipster regulars. There's an excellent booze list; go for draft sake or a craft-beer tasting flight dominated by BC favorite Driftwood Brewing. Foodwise, the Koerner Organic Burger is a staple but also try the crunchy UBC Farm Salad, largely sourced from the university's own nearby farm. (604-827-1443; www.koerners.ca; 6371 Crescent Rd; 11:30am-9pm Mon-Wed, to midnight Thu & Fri summer, extended hours in term time; 99B-Line)

49th Parallel Coffee

COFFEE

15 Map p108, G3

Kitsilano's favorite coffeeshop hangout. Sit with the locals in the glass-enclosed outdoor seating area (handy in deluge-prone Raincouver) and slowly sip your latte while scoffing as many own-brand Lucky's Doughnuts as you can manage; just because they're artisanal, doesn't mean you should have only one. Need a recommendation? Try an apple-bacon fritter. Or two. (www.49thparallelroasters.com; 2198 W 4th Ave; 7am-7pm Mon-Thu, to 8pm Fri-Sun; 4)

Understand
Public Art

Vanier Park's Artsy Side

The waterfront park that houses three museums also has an artistic edge. It's the home of the annual and highly popular Bard on the Beach Shakespeare festival but it also include a hulking artwork that dominates the skyline. Almost 5m high, *Gate to the Northwest Passage* is a weathered steel square that many visitors use to frame their photos of the mountains across the water. But this landmark work isn't the city's only brush with public art.

Artworks Abound

Vancouver has a vigorous public art program and you'll likely spot challenging installations, decorative apartment-building adornments and sometimes puzzling sculptures dotted throughout the city. Check www.vancouver.ca/publicart for an online registry of works and some handy maps, or pick up the excellent book *Public Art in Vancouver: Angels Among Lions*, by John Steil and Aileen Stalker. It has photos and information on more than 500 works around the city, divided into neighborhoods. Also, check the website of the **Vancouver Biennale** (www.vancouverbiennale.com), a massive public-art showcase, staged in two-year chunks, that brings monumental, often challenging, installations to the city's streets from artists around the world. The website shows where to find these works and plot your own walking tour.

Most-photographed Works

Among the public artworks to look out for in Vancouver are the 14 smiling, oversized bronze figures near the shoreline of English Bay, which form one of Canada's most-photographed art installations; the five wrecked cars piled on top of a cedar tree trunk near Science World; the pixilated-looking orca alongside downtown's Convention Centre; the towering neon cross at Clark Dr and E 6th Ave; the silver replica of a freight shed on piles on the Coal Harbour seawall; and, of course, the quirky white-painted poodle on Main St that locals either love or loathe.

Entertainment

Bard on the Beach
PERFORMING ARTS

16 Map p108, H2

Watching Shakespeare being performed while the sun sets against the mountains beyond the tented stage is a Vancouver summertime highlight. There are usually three of Shakespeare's plays, plus one Bard-related work (*Rosencrantz and Guildenstern are Dead,* for example), to choose from during the run. Q&A talks are staged after Tuesday-night performances, and there are opera, fireworks and wine-tasting nights throughout the season. (604-739-0559; www.bardonthebeach.org; Vanier Park, 1695 Whyte Ave; tickets $20-57; Jun-Sep; 22)

Kitsilano Showboat
CONCERT VENUE

17 Map p108, G2

An 80-year-old tradition that generations of locals know and love, this alfresco waterfront stage near Kits Pool offers free shows and concerts in summer. Grab a bleacher-style seat facing the sunset-illuminating North Shore mountains and prepare for singers, musicians, dancers or more; check the online schedule to see what's coming up. A great way to mix and mingle with the chatty locals. (604-734-7332; www.kitsilanoshowboat.com; 2300 Cornwall Ave; admission free; 7pm Mon, Wed, Fri & Sat mid-Jun–mid-Aug; 22)

Shopping

Kidsbooks
BOOKS

18 Map p108, G3

From *Squishy McFluff* to *The Great Big Dinosaur*, this huge child-friendly store – reputedly Canada's biggest kids' bookshop – has thousands of novels, picture books and anything else you can think of to keep your bookish sprogs quiet. There are also regular readings by visiting authors and a selection of quality toys and games to provide a break from all that strenuous page-turning. (www.kidsbooks. ca; 2557 W Broadway; 9:30am-6pm Mon-Thu & Sat, 9:30am-9pm Fri, 11am-6pm Sun; 9)

Silk Road Tea
TEA

19 Map p108, H3

Plunging into the scalding hot Kitsilano tea wars (there are two rival purveyors nearby), this new branch of Victoria's favorite fancy tea emporium combines superbly friendly staff with a lip-smacking array of hundreds of leafy varieties. Peruse the top-notch green, herbal and wellness teas and pick up a super-cool teapot to add to your suitcase-packing woes. (778-379-8481; www.silkroadteastore.com; 2066 W 4th Ave; 10am-7pm Mon-Sat, to 6pm Sun; 4)

Stepback
HOMEWARES

20 Map p108, F3

When your to-buy list includes taxidermy, vintage typewriters and retro suitcases, this brilliantly curated, highly browsable shop is the place for you. Among the new and used trinkets, homewares and accessories, look out for enamel kitchenware, leather journals and yesteryear postcards of old Vancouver and beyond. There are usually far more people looking than buying; this place almost feels like a little museum. (☎604-731-7525; 2936 W Broadway; ⊙11am-5:30pm Tue-Fri, 10am-6pm Sat, noon-5pm Sun; 🚊9)

Kitsilano Farmers Market

MARKET

21 🔒 Map p108, G3

Kitsilano's best excuse to get out and hang with the locals, this seasonal farmers market is one of the city's most popular. Arrive early for the best selection and you'll have the pick of freshly plucked local fruit and veg, such as sweet strawberries or spectacularly flavorful heirloom tomatoes. You'll likely never want to shop in a mainstream supermarket again. (www.eatlocal.org; Kitsilano Community Centre, 2690 Larch St; ⊙10am-2pm Sun mid-May–mid-Oct; 🚊4)

Zulu Records

MUSIC

22 🔒 Map p108, H3

Kitsilano's fave indie music store has downsized from its double storefront

Kitsilano Farmers Market

but it's still easy to blow an afternoon here sifting the new and used recordings and hard-to-find imports. There's a scuzzy-carpeted, *High Fidelity* ambiance here; ask the music-nerd staff for tips on local live music and check the $2 boxes for that rare Pia Zadora record you've been looking for. (☎604-738-3232; www.zulurecords.com; 1972 W 4th Ave; ⊙10:30am-7pm Mon-Wed, 10:30am-9pm Thu & Fri, 9:30am-6:30pm Sat, noon-6pm Sun; 🚊4)

Top Sights
Capilano Suspension Bridge Park

Getting There

🚌 236 from North Vancouver's Lonsdale Quay (arrival point for the Sea service from downtown Vancouver) stops across the street from Capilano.

One of Metro Vancouver's most-visited attractions, it's jam-packed with tour buses in summer. But there's a reason everyone's coming: that jelly-leg-triggering suspension bridge over the roiling, tree-flanked waters of Capilano Canyon is one of the region's most memorable highlights. There's more, though; a host of extra attractions have been added to this scenery-hugging park in recent years.

Bridge

Starting life as a simple rope-and-plank span in 1880, the bridge's current steel cable iteration stretches 137m: wide enough to fly two Boeing 747s wing-to-wing underneath (strangely, no one has tried this). Swaying gently as they walk across (unless a group of deliberately heavy-footed teenagers is stomping nearby), most first-timers steady themselves on the cable 'handrail' but let go as they adapt to the leg-wobbling sensation.

Park

The bridge is the star attraction but there's much more to keep you occupied here. Check the outdoor historic displays and First Nations totem poles before heading across. And once you're on the other side, explore the trails and wooden walkways that take you deeper into the forest. Also peruse the kid-friendly displays on the area's flora and fauna, from woodpeckers to banana slugs.

Canopy Walk

On this side of the bridge, you can also access **Treetops Adventure** (pictured), a 200m-long series of smaller suspension bridges and walkways strung high up between the trees. Cleverly designed to avoid damaging the trees it's attached to, it'll give you a squirrel's-eye view of the rainforest.

Cliffwalk

Head back over to other side of the bridge (you probably won't need to hold on so tightly this time), turn left and look for the entrance to Cliffwalk, another included-with-admission extra. Descend the steps and you'll find yourself on a lofty steel bridge walkway clinging tenaciously to the rockside and overlooking the watery canyon below. The scariest part? The glass-bottomed sections that make your legs tingle in protest.

☎ 604-985-7474

www.capbridge.com

3735 Capilano Rd, North Vancouver

adult/child $40/12

🕑 8:30am-8pm Jun-Aug, reduced hours off-season

🅿 👫

🚌 236

☑ Top Tips

▶ Arrive soon after opening time to avoid the summer crowds.

▶ A free shuttle bus runs from downtown to the park's entrance.

▶ Grouse Mountain is 10 minutes north on the same 236 bus route.

✗ Take a Break

Grab a hot chocolate on the other side of the bridge at the park's rustic **Dr Wood's Cabin** (☎ 604-985-7474; www. capbridge.com; 🕑 8:30am-8pm Jun-Aug, reduced hours off-season; 🚌 236).

The Best of
Vancouver

Vancouver's Best Walks

Vancouver's Best...

First Nations totem poles in Stanley Park (p24)
SONGQUAN DENG/SHUTTERSTOCK ©

Best Walks
Downtown Grand Tour

🏃 The Walk

The bustling heart of Vancouver city center is an eminently walkable street grid of stores, coffeeshops and dining options. But there are also more than a few grand buildings and scenic sights to whip out your camera for. Take your time and see what you can find.

Start Canada Place; 🚇 SkyTrain Waterfront

Finish Bella Gelateria; 🚇 SkyTrain Waterfront

Length 3km; one hour

✕ Take a Break

There are plenty of coffeeshop pit-stop options on Granville St and beyond. For lunch, consider the sun-kissed patio of the **Gallery Café** (p37) or the freshly made salad-and-sandwich offerings at **Tractor** (p36).

Olympic Cauldron

❶ Canada Place

Start at postcard-favorite **Canada Place** (p34), giving your camera free rein. You can walk along the outer promenade to watch the floatplanes diving onto the water.

❷ Convention Centre West Building

Next, stroll to the adjacent **Convention Centre West Building**. Peruse the eye-catching artworks outside, including a 'pixelated orca' sculpture by Douglas Coupland.

❸ Olympic Cauldron

You're now in **Jack Poole Plaza**. Check out the towering Olympic Cauldron, a landmark reminder of the 2010 Olympic Winter Games.

❹ Granville & W Georgia Streets

Head southwest along Howe St, turn left onto W Hastings St and then right onto store-lined Granville St. You'll pass the **Pacific Centre**, downtown's biggest mall. Get your bearings at the intersection of Granville & W Georgia Sts.

ALISON RIDGWAY/LONELY PLANET IMAGES ©

5 Vancouver Art Gallery

Check out the shops around here or nip one block over to the **Vancouver Art Gallery** (p28) for a culture fix. Return later to really immerse yourself.

6 Vancouver Public Library

From here, stroll southeast a couple of blocks to the Colosseum-like **Vancouver Public Library**. The glass-enclosed atrium is a perfect for a coffee.

7 Robson & Burrard Streets

Head northwest along Robson St, the city's main shopping promenade. There are many restaurants here, so make note of some dinner options.

8 Fairmont Hotel Vancouver

Duck into the grand **Fairmont Hotel Vancouver.** There are photos on one wall showing the historic building's construction and former incarnations.

9 Christ Church Cathedral

Across the street is Vancouver's favorite **cathedral** (p35), still here despite 1970s moves to demolish it. Check out its new stained-glass bell tower.

10 Bella Gelateria

Amble down Burrard St with the mountains ahead of you, passing the art deco **Marine Building** (p34). You're almost back at Canada Place, but stop for a treat at **Bella Gelateria** (p37) first.

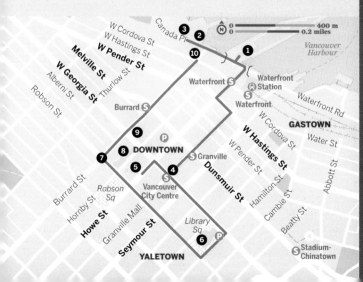

Best Walks
Gastown
Bar Crawl

🏃 The Walk

The Granville Strip lures a party-hard crowd with its mainstream bars and noisy nightclubs. But you're much more likely to meet the locals in Gastown. The historic, brick-paved neighborhood is lined with great places to drink, without having to walk (or crawl) too far.

Start Steamworks Brew Pub; 🚇 SkyTrain Waterfront

Finish Alibi Room

Length 1km; time depends how fast you drink...

✕ Take a Break

There are plenty of places to fuel up in and around this area. Consider the finger-licking Mexican-inspired menu at **Tacofino** (p54) or a coffee pit stop with the hipsters at **Revolver** (p57).

Six Acres

❶ Steamworks Brew Pub

Start your crawl on the edge of Gastown with a fortifying oatmeal stout at cavernous **Steamworks Brew Pub** (p58), one of Vancouver's few brewpubs.

❷ Gassy Jack Statue

Incline left onto Water St and amble downhill towards Maple Tree Sq. You'll find a **statue** (p53) of a slightly stooped man atop a whiskey barrel. Near this spot, John Deighton's (Gassy Jack) first pub triggered the settlement that later became Vancouver.

❸ Guilt & Co

Across the square, duck underground to **Guilt & Co** (p57), a local favorite. There's often live music here, as well as board games and a great array of bottled beer.

❹ Six Acres

Back outside, nip back across the square to **Six Acres** (p56), one of Gastown's coziest hangouts. You'll be tempted

CANADA/ALAMY STOCK PHOTO ©

to stick around, but the spirit of Gassy will soon be calling you back to the streets.

⑤ Irish Heather

Cross Carrall St and duck into the **Irish Heather** (p58). The best spot in town for a Guinness, it also has a whiskey bar out back where you can fully indulge.

⑥ Diamond

If you're still walking by this stage, head back onto Carrall and take the first right onto Powell St. The street sign will point you to the unassuming stairwell leading to the lovely **Diamond** (p58), a great spot for perfect cocktails.

⑦ Alibi Room

Head back out and take nearby Alexander St eastwards. Within a couple of minutes you'll be at the **Alibi Room** (p56). This is Vancouver's favorite craft-beer bars and a 'frat bat' of sample brews is recommended. Check the specials board for top British Columbia (BC) beers.

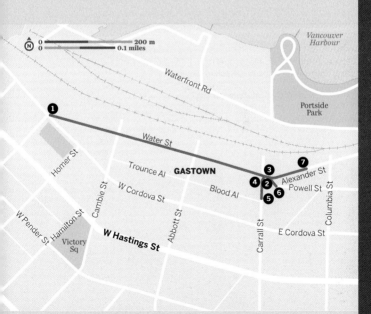

Best
Dining Out

DARRYL BROOKS/SHUTTERSTOCK ©

Vancouver has an amazing array of generally good value dine-out options: top-drawer sushi joints, clamorous Chinese restaurants, inviting indie eateries and a fresh-picked farm-to-table scene are all on the menu. You don't have to be a local to indulge: follow your tastebuds and dinner will become a talked-about highlight of your visit.

Seafood

One reason Vancouver has great sushi is the larder of top-table seafood available right off the boat. Given the length of British Columbia's coastline, it's no surprise most restaurants (whether Asian, Mexican, West Coast or French) find plenty of menu space for goodies such as salmon, halibut, spot prawns and freshly shucked oysters. If you're a seafood fan, you'll be in your element; even fish and chips is typically excellent. Start your aquatic odyssey at the seafood vendors on and around Granville Island.

Farm to Table

Vancouver now fully embraces its regional food and farm producers. Restaurants can't wait to tell you about the Fraser Valley duck and foraged morels they've just discovered. Seasonal is key, and you'll see lots of local specials on menus. Adding to the feast, some restaurants showcase local cheese producers, and most have also taken their BC love affair to the drinks list: Okanagan wines have been a staple here for years but BC craft beer is the current darling of thirsty Vancouver locavores.

Asian Smorgasbord

Vancouver is home to the best Asian dining scene outside Asia. From authentic sushi and ramen spots to Korean and Vietnamese street food and fine dining, as well as a richly varied Chinese scene that runs from dim sum to dragon's beard candy, you'll be spoilt for choice here. Adventurous foodies should also dive into the local summer night-market scene.

Sushi selection

Best International Dining

Vij's Newly relocated, the city's favorite Indian restaurant. (p95)

Ask for Luigi Railtown charmer with delightful Italian dishes. (p54)

Mr Red Cafe Revelatory northern Vietnamse cuisine. (p112)

Best West Coast Dining

Forage Showcase of farm-to-table West Coast dining. (p36)

Tacofino West Coast taco hotspot in a great Gastown setting. (p54)

Fable Kitsilano's favorite farm-to-table restaurant. (p113)

Best Budget Dining

Bestie German sausages and fries in a fun hipster haunt in Chinatown. (p55)

La Taqueria Pinche Taco Shop Four tacos for around $10, with a side order of super-friendly service. (p94)

Tony's Fish & Oyster Cafe Great-value Granville Island seafood, popular with locals. (p75)

Best
Drinking &
Nightlife

Vancouverites spend a lot of time drinking. And while BC has a tasty wine sector and is undergoing an artisan distilling surge, it's the regional craft-beer scene that keeps many quaffers merry. For a night out with local-made libations, join savvy drinkers supping in Gastown, Main St and around Commercial Dr – then hit a club or two.

Craft Beer

BC is Canada's craft-beer capital with almost 200 producers, including dozens in Vancouver. You can plan an easy stroll (or stumble) around inviting clusters of microbrewery tasting rooms on and around Main St or the northern end of Commercial Dr. Most city bars also showcase regional brews; look out for locally loved producers like Four Winds, Powell Street, Central City and Main Street. For more on the local beer scene, visit www.camravancouver.ca.

Wine & Liquor

BC wine launched Vancouver's love of local-made booze and several cool wine bars have popped up in recent years to satisfy thirsty oenophiles. But the cocktails scene has also started impressing here, with a selection of drinking joints, from traditional to quirky, joining the nightlife fray. Craft distilleries are the latest wave; look out for recently opened spots on your visit. And don't forget that new happy-hour rules mean you can afford to be adventurous.

Clubbing

While downtown's Granville Strip draws the barely clad booties of mainstream clubbers, there are other, less limelight-hogging areas catering to just about every peccadillo. Cover charges run from $5 to $20 ('the ladies' often get in free before 11pm) and dress codes are frequently smart-casual – ripped jeans and sportswear will not endear you to bouncers keen to find reasons to send people home. Bring ID: most clubs accept over-19s but some want you to be over 25. You can join the VIP lists (no waiting, no cover) at the websites of individual clubs or via www.clubzone.com.

Granville Island Brewing Taproom (p77)

Best for Beer

Steamworks Brew Pub Large Gastown brewpub offering housemade beers, including an excellent oatmeal stout. (p58)

Granville Island Brewing Taproom Try the label's famous brews including Cypress Honey Lager, Lions Winter Ale and Black Notebook beers. (p77)

Storm Crow Alehouse Large nerd pub with board games and sci-fi props on the walls. (p97)

Alibi Room Superb BC and beyond craft-beer selection wrapped in a friendly tavern vibe. (p56)

Irish Heather Great place for sausage and mash with a pint of Guinness. (p58)

Best for Wine & Cocktails

Liberty Distillery Craft liquor maker with a top tasting room. (p65)

Diamond Alluring upstairs room with perfect, classic cocktails. (p58)

Shameful Tiki Room Main St's authentic-looking tiki bar, with vintage cocktails to match. (p85)

Artisan Sake Maker Granville Island's own sake producer makes smooth and subtle concoctions. (p76)

Best
Entertainment

SERGE BACHLAKOV/SHUTTERSTOCK ©

You'll never run out of options if you're looking for a good show here. Vancouver is packed with stage-based activities from high- to low-brow, perfect for those craving a play one night, a movie the next and a rocking live music show after that. Ask the locals for tips and they'll likely point out grassroots happenings you never knew existed.

Live Music

Superstar acts hit the stages at sports stadiums while smaller indie bands crowd tight spaces around town. Local independent record stores offer the low-down on venues and acts to catch. Vancouver has a wide array of musical tastes and, with some digging, you'll also find jazz, folk, classical and opera here.

Live Theater

Vancouver has a long history of theater. The **Arts Club Theatre Company** (www.artsclub.com) is the city's leading troupe – with three stages around the city – but **Bard on the Beach** is an annual summer tradition among locals: Shakespeare plays performed in tents in Vanier Park. Look out for performing arts festivals as well, especially January's **PuSh Festival** (www.pushfestival. ca) and September's **Vancouver Fringe Festival** (www.vancouverfringe.com).

Movies

While some independent movie theaters have closed in recent years, there are still plenty of places to catch blockbusters as well as a couple of downtown art-house cinemas for those who like subtitles rather than car chases: check out www.cinemaclock.com to see what's on. Also consider the popular **Vancouver International Film Festival** (www.viff.org) plus smaller film fests like the **DOXA Documentary Film Festival** (www.doxafestival.ca) and **Vancouver Asian Film Festival** (www.vaff.org).

Dance

Vancouver is a major center for Canadian dance, offering an esoteric array of classical ballet and edgy contemporary fare. The city is home to more than 30 professional companies as well as many internationally recognized choreographers. Check out downtown's **Dance Centre** and July's **Dancing on the Edge festival** (www.dancingontheedge.org).

Lorraine Klaasen, Vancouver International Jazz Festival (p137)

Best for Live Music

Commodore Ballroom
Springy-floored legendary music venue. (p40)

Rickshaw Theatre Top Chinatown venue for indie and punk acts. (p58)

Backstage Lounge Granville Island bar hosting local bands. (p78)

Uva Wine & Cocktail Bar Live jazz on Saturday nights. (p38)

Best Live Theaters

Stanley Theatre Heritage theater, staging plays and musicals. (p99)

Bard on the Beach Shakespeare plays in waterfront tents. (p116)

Theatre Under the Stars Smile-triggering summertime musicals on an alfresco Stanley Park stage. (p41)

Best
Outdoor Activities

Vancouver's variety of outdoorsy activities is a huge hook: you can ski in the morning and hit the beach in the afternoon; hike or bike scenic forests; windsurf along the coastline; or kayak to your heart's content – and it will be content, with grand mountain views as your backdrop. There's also a full menu of spectator sports to catch.

LISANDRA MELO/SHUTTERSTOCK ©

Cycling & Hiking

Vancouver is a cycle-friendly city with a network of designated urban routes and a new public bikshare scheme. For maps and resources, see www.vancouver.ca/cycling. There's also a very active mountain-biking community on the North Shore; start your research via www.nsmba.ca. Hiking-wise, you'll find trails in green spaces throughout the region – visit www.vancouvertrails.com for options.

On the Water

It's hard to beat the joy of a sunset kayak around the coastline here, but hitting the water isn't only about paddling: there are also plenty of opportunities to surf, kiteboard and stand-up paddleboard, especially along the Kitsilano shoreline.

Best Outdoor Action

Stanley Park Breath-takingly scenic walking, jogging and cycling trail around this park's seawall. (p24)

Ecomarine Paddlesport Centres Perfect sunset paddling activity on False Creek. (p73)

Best Spectator Sports

Vancouver Canucks City's fave NHL hockey passion. (p42)

BC Lions Canadian Football League team, playing at BC Place. (p78)

Vancouver Whitecaps The city's Major League Soccer team. (p78)

Best
Parks & Gardens

Vancouver's sparkling natural setting is a major reason many visitors fall for this city. Plunge into activities at beaches, mountain promontories and tree-lined trails, both urban and on the city's wilder fringes.

Top Green Spaces

There are green spots galore in Vancouver, from manicured botanical gardens to wilder swaths where you'll feel as close as possible to nature. And while Stanley Park – Canada's favorite urban green space – is justly revered, there are many more outdoorsy places to look out for.

Seawall Trail

Vancouver has a spectacular seawall trail linking more than 20km of waterfront. It weaves from downtown's Canada Place through Stanley Park and out to the University of BC. Don't miss the False Creek stretch for its public art.

Beaches

You're never far from great beaches in Vancouver, including the sandy Kits Beach and English Bay beach plus quieter gems like Third Beach and Spanish Banks. Add a picnic for the perfect visit.

DOMINIK ECKELT/GETTY IMAGES ©

Best Parks & Gardens

Stanley Park Start on the seawall and add the tranquil interior trails. (p24)

Queen Elizabeth Park Vancouver's other big city park, with sparkling downtown views. (p94)

VanDusen Botanical Garden The city's favorite manicured green space. (p88)

UBC Botanical Garden Popular campus-based garden attraction. (p110)

Best
Shopping

Vancouver's retail scene has developed dramatically in recent years. Hit Robson St's mainstream chains, then discover the hip, independent shops of Gastown, Main St and Commercial Dr. Granville Island is stuffed with artsy stores and studios, while South Granville and Kitsilano's 4th Ave serve up a wide range of ever-tempting boutiques.

Independent Fashion

Vancouver has a bulging shopping bag of independent stores with well-curated collections from local and international designers. Peruse the main drags of Gastown, South Granville and Kitsilano's 4th Ave for one-of-a-kind boutiques. Keep your eyes peeled for pop-up shops and check the pages of *Vancouver* magazine and the *Georgia Straight* for retail happenings such as Gastown's 'shop hops' – seasonal evenings of late openings with a party-like vibe. Before you arrive, also peruse Vancouver fashion blogs including www.aliciafashionista.com and www.tovogueorbust.com.

Arts & Crafts

The city's arts scene dovetails invitingly with its retail sector. There are dozens of intriguing private galleries, showcasing everything from contemporary Canadian art to authentic First Nations carvings and jewelry. There are also opportunities to buy art from indie galleries on Main and from the many artisan studios on Granville Island. In addition, there are dozens of arts and crafts fairs throughout the year; check local listings publications or www.gotcraft.com for upcoming events.

Souvenirs

For decades, visitors to Vancouver have been returning home with suitcases full of maple-sugar cookies and vacuum-packed smoked salmon. But it doesn't have to be this way. Consign your steam-clock fridge magnet to the garbage and aim for authentic First Nations art or silver jewelry; a book on Vancouver's eye-popping history (*Sensational Vancouver* by Eve Lazarus, for example); some delightful locally made pottery from Granville Island; or a quirky Vancouver-designed T-shirt from the fashion stores on Main St.

Robson St shop-window displays

Best Indie Shops

Regional Assembly of Text Vancouver's favorite hangout for fans of stationery and typewriting your own letters. (p85)

Paper Hound Perfect little downtown second-hand book store. (p42)

Neptoon Records Great vinyl and CD selection in a *High Fidelity*–like setting. (p85)

Smoking Lily Beloved array of hip, locally designed womenswear. (p85)

Best for Arts & Crafts

Gallery of BC Ceramics Excellent selection of locally made artisan pottery. (p79)

Coastal Peoples Fine Arts Gallery Top Gastown spot for buying authentic First Nations works. (p61)

Crafthouse Showcasing a wide array of arts and crafts produced throughout the region. (p81)

Best Vintage Shopping

Eastside Flea Regular used and vintage market on Main St. (p60)

Community Thrift & Vintage Great selection of vintage clothing. (p60)

Stepback Museum-like store with new and vintage knickknacks. (p116)

Best
Festivals

While July and August are peak months for Vancouver festivals, the city has a year-round roster of events that should give you some entertaining options no matter what time of year you're here. Check local listings publications like the Georgia Straight (www.straight.com) to see what's coming up.

Art

Cultural festivals have been a big draw among Vancouverites for decades with huge annual events showcasing everything from film to fringe theater and from Shakespeare plays to art studio open houses. But it's not all about big events. The city is also a hotbed of small-scale grassroots happenings which only the locals seem to know about. Check local listing papers for events.

Music

If music is more your bag, summer in the city offers stages – many of them outdoors – where jazz, folk, classical and beyond are performed. Book ahead for tickets to the top shows at many of these events or just join the crowds for the free alfresco shows: peruse festival websites before you arrive to plot your schedule. If you have the time and really want to immerse yourself in an event, consider volunteering: you'll typically receive free passes to other shows when you're not herding the crowds during your volunteer shifts.

Community Events

The mother of all Vancouver community fests is the annual July 1 **Canada Day** celebration at Canada Place. But there are also smaller Canada Day events at Granville Island and throughout the region and they're a great way to witness how proud of their country the locals are. Expect maple-leaf tattoos, impromptu 'O Canada' renditions and end-of-day fireworks' displays. But there's more: check local listings for party-like open-to-all annual events around the city, celebrating the local Greek, Italian, Caribbean and Japanese communities.

Food & Booze

Vancouverites love events where they can hang out together and drink and dine. The city has many food and drink festivals – from large annual events themed around wine and craft beer to smaller happenings.

Japanese drumming, Powell Street Festival

Best Arts Festivals

Vancouver International Film Festival (www.viff. org) From late September, this huge annual event showcases great movies from Canada and around the world.

Vancouver International Jazz Festival (www. coastaljazz.ca) June's jazz-tastic event includes top performances and a wide range of free shows around the city.

Eastside Culture Crawl (www.culturecrawl.ca) November's weekend-long open house for hundreds of artist studios is the city's best grass-roots art event.

Best Food & Drink Festivals

Vancouver International Wine Festival (www. vanwinefest.ca) One of Canada's oldest annual wine events profiles the grape-based production of a different country or region every year.

Vancouver Beer Week (www.vancouvercraft beerweek.com) A newer but wildly popular annual event during which the region's amazing craft beer is given its just desserts.

Best Community Festivals

Powell Street Festival (www.powellstreet festival.com) In and around the old Japantown area, this excellent festival celebrates all things Japanese.

Italian Day (www.italian day.ca) On Commercial Dr, this clamorous day-long event covers all the food, music and partying bases.

Best
Gay & Lesbian

Vancouver's gay and lesbian scene is part of the city's culture rather than a subsection of it. The legalization of same-sex marriage here several years ago makes it a popular spot for those who want to tie the knot in scenic style. But if you just want to kick back and have a great time, this is also Canada's top gay-tastic party city.

CARTERDAYNE/GETTY IMAGES ©

West End

The West End's Davie St is the center of Vancouver's gay scene. Sometimes called the Gay Village, this is Canada's largest 'gayborhood' and it's marked by rainbow flags, hand-holding locals and pink-painted bus shelters. There's a full menu of scene-specific pubs and bars, and it's a warm and welcoming district for everyone, gay or straight. Find the perfect spot sitting at a street-side cafe pretending to check your phone while actually checking out the passing talent; you can expect to make friends pretty quickly here. In addition, Vancouver's Commercial Dr is a traditional center of the lesbian scene.

Pride Week

Showing how far the scene has progressed since the days when Vancouver's gay community was forced to stay in the closet, Pride Week is now Canada's biggest annual gay celebration. Staged around the first week of August, the centerpiece is the parade – a huge street fiesta of disco-pumping floats, drum-beating marching bands and gyrating, barely clad locals dancing through the streets as if they've been waiting all year for the opportunity.

In 2016, Justin Trudeau marched in the parade, becoming the first Canadian prime minister to do so. The parade is only the most visual evidence of Pride Week; this is also the time to dive into galas, drag contests, all-night parties and a queer film fest. During the same week, East Vancouver's annual Dyke March concludes with a festival and beer garden in Grandview Park on Commercial Dr.

Nightlife

You're unlikely to run out of places to hang with the locals in Vancouver's lively gay scene. Davie St, in particular, is home to diverse gay-driven bars and dance clubs. But it's not all about the West End: look out for gay-friendly nights at clubs and bars around the city. Peruse your options at www.gay vancouver.net/nightlife.

Vancouver Pride Parade

Best Gay & Lesbian Bars & Businesses

1181 Smooth lounge bar with slick clientele. (p39)

Little Sister's Book & Art Emporium Catch up on your reading at this local legend bookstore. (p43)

Fountainhead Pub laid-back, beer-friendly gay community pub. (p40)

Pumpjack Pub Some-times raucous spot, great for making new friends. (p40)

Delany's Coffee House Grab a strong caffeine hit at this Denman St coffeeshop with street-side tables. (p40)

Best
For Kids

Family-friendly Vancouver is stuffed with attractions for kids – and there are also plenty of outdoor activities to tire them out before bedtime. Several festivals are especially kid-tastic, and local transportation experiences, including SeaBus and SkyTrain, are highlights for many youngsters.

Science & Nature

From space and science centers to outdoor attractions that illuminate the flora and fauna of the region, Vancouver has plenty of options for suitably-inclined youngsters. And once you're done exploring the well-known attractions, save time to simply hit the trails for a wander: Stanley Park is the perfect spot for explorers keen to dive into the natural world.

Animal Encounters

Kids from other countries are often wide-eyed with wonder when they spot their first racoon in a park here. If you're lucky, they might also see deer, eagles and brightly-colored starfish. Make sure your family is bear-aware if you're venturing from the city and take this opportunity to teach your youngsters not to chase or otherwise bother critters in their natural habitats.

History Huggers

If your children love museums, Vancouver has several attractions with a kid-friendly vibe. Vanier Park is home to three diverse museums catering to those interested in everything from maritime heritage to colorful local history.

Sea turtle, Vancouver Aquarium (p35)

Best Museums & Attractions

Science World A hands-on science center that's mastered the art of teaching kids through fun. (p72)

HR MacMillan Space Centre Perfect for astronomically-minded children, with plenty of push-button games and activities. (p111)

Capilano Suspension Bridge Park After inching over the canyon on the (deliberately) wobbly wooden bridge, take some short trails through the forest to learn about the towering trees and local critters. (p119)

BC Sports Hall of Fame & Museum Traces the region's sporting past via kid-friendly displays and activities. (p72)

Best for Nature Fans

Bloedel Conservatory A delightful way to commune with hundreds of exotic birds; ask nicely and staff will let your child feed several at once from a bowl. (p94)

Stanley Park Nature House Your kids can quiz the friendly volunteers about the park's flora and fauna and partake of birdwatching tours, especially in summer. (p34)

Vancouver Aquarium Offers otters, iridescent jellyfish and dolphins to view, plus trainer encounters if your kids are keen on behind-the-scenes tours. (p35)

Beaty Biodiversity Museum Head to the back of this UBC museum for plenty of kid-focused exhibits and activities. (p110)

Best
Green Initiatives

It's hard to see Vancouver as anything but a green city: its dense forests and verdant, rain-fed plant life make nature an ever-present fact of life here. But beyond the breathtaking visuals, how does the city measure up to its environmental responsibilities? And – just as importantly – what can Vancouver-bound visitors do to reduce their own eco-footprint in the region without turning their vacation into a monastic, fun-free zone?

City Foraging

For a cool introduction to the edible plants growing alongside us, book ahead for a tour with Vancouver's **Forager Foundation** (www.foragertours.com). Promoting traditional methods of gathering food and medicine, the nonprofit organization runs illuminating tours – often including Stanley Park – for curious locals and visitors.

Tree Hugging

For many, fall is the best time to hang out with the trees in Vancouver. Burnished copper, pumpkin-orange, deep candy-apple red: the seemingly infinite colors of autumn under cloudless blue skies make this a fave time of year for many locals. If you're here in October, charge up your camera, slip into comfortable walking shoes and hunt down the following pigment-popping locations.

Make a beeline for **Stanley Park**. Hit the seawall – by bike or on foot – to find rusty amber hues and Japanese maple reds studding the evergreen Douglas firs. Across town at **Queen Elizabeth Park**, weave uphill among the trees from the Cambie St entrance. On a fine day, you'll also have one of the best wide-angled vistas over the glass-towered city, framed by ice-frosted mountains.

It's not all parks, of course. Many older residential neighborhoods here resemble spilled paintboxes of color every fall. The West End is striped with residential streets where fall-flavored trees mix with brightly painted heritage houses, while sections of Mt Pleasant's 10th Ave are like a walk-through kaleidoscope of century-old chestnut trees.

Fall foliage, Stanley Park (p24)

Green Shoots

Many Vancouver green initiatives are at the grass-roots community level and one of our favorites is the city's **Pop-up Library** phenomenon. Several neighborhoods across Vancouver have built their own pop-up mini-libraries for all to use. One of the largest is the St George Sharing Library, a double-shelved covered table a few steps from the intersection of East 10th Ave and St George St. It's always bulging with well-used paperbacks, including the occasional Lonely Planet guidebook.

Vancouver's **Fruit Tree Project Society** (www.vancouverfruittree.com) deploys a green army of volunteers to harvest treats that would otherwise rot on trees around the city. Collecting hundreds of kilos of fruit every year, the goodies – typically including plums, apples, pears and grapes – are redistributed to those in need around the city.

Best Green Attractions

Stanley Park Vancouver's (and possibly Canada's) greatest green space). (p24)

Stanley Park Nature House Friendly introduction to the region's flora and fauna. (p34)

UBC Botanical Garden Lovely garden attractions that combine themed areas with swaths of rustic forest. (p110)

Best
Museums &
Galleries

While outdoor action monopolizes much of the spare time of local Vancouverites, there are also some top-notch cultural attractions if you love rubbing your chin more than rubbing your calves. Check local listings publications such as the Georgia Straight (www.straight.com) for events, opening and happenings.

KLAUS LANG/GETTY IMAGES ©

Museums

With its own local history museum regaling locals and visitors with the city's colorful story – plus other museums themed around space, seafaring and biodiversity, as well as a popular science center – Vancouver has more than enough options if you're looking for some indoor cultural or educational action. The best of the bunch? Head to the University of BC for Western Canada's best anthropology museum. Check the websites of each institution for upcoming temporary exhibitions.

Galleries

Downtown's main city art gallery is a highly popular cultural magnet and the best time to visit is during its FUSE evening events, when locals sip wine, watch live performances and peruse the exhibitions. But Vancouver's art scene is mostly a highly inventive grassroots affair. Do some online homework before you arrive and check out what's coming up.

Best Museum & Galleries

Museum of Anthropology Brilliantly presented repository of cultural artifacts from BC and around the world. (p104)

Vancouver Art Gallery Housed in a landmark heritage building, the city's most important gallery leads the local art scene. (p28)

Museum of Vancouver Engaging Vanier Park attraction telling the story of the city in several fascinating galleries. (p110)

Best
Architecture

When the first version of Vancouver burned to the ground during the Great Fire of 1886, it seemed prudent to use brick and stone for the new town that emerged from the ashes. While some of the buildings from this era survive, Vancouver's latter-day skyline is dominated by shimmering towers, reflected in one of its nicknames: City of Glass.

Historic Treasures

Every year, **Heritage Vancouver** (www.heritage vancouver.org) produces a list of 10 historic structures, streets or neighborhoods it believes are under threat of destruction. The list has recently included St Paul's Hospital, the South Granville apartment district, Bloedel Conservatory, Pantages Theatre (which was actually demolished soon after it appeared on the list) and the vintage neon signs that dot the city. The nonprofit organization's motto is 'demolition is forever' and it advocates swift preservation – before it's too late.

MICHAEL WHEATLEY/AGEFOTOSTOCK ©

Best Buildings

Marine Building Vancouver's favorite art deco masterpiece. (p34)

City Hall The 1930s-built landmark is studded with art deco flourishes. (p100)

Canada Place The city's convention center and cruise-ship terminal is the city's most striking waterfront landmark. (p34)

Roedde House A house museum reminder of the wood-built mansions that once lined the West End. (p34)

Science World A shimmering silver dome built for the Expo '86 world exposition. (p72)

Christ Church Cathedral Downtown's favorite historic church, complete with handsome new bell tower. (p35)

Best
For Free

There are plenty of sights and activities to enjoy in Vancouver without opening your wallet. Follow the locals and check local listings and you'll soon be perusing art shows, noodling around parks and taking in a gratis tour or two.

Gratis Sights & Activities

Check out the free-entry architectural landmarks covered in the Architecture section (p145; including two art deco buildings). And consider the free summer shows on the Kitslano waterfront. There's also a free-entry nature center in Stanley Park, a steam train display in Yaletown and a gratis art gallery at the University of BC.

Discounts Galore

The **Vancouver Art Gallery** offers by-donation entry on Tuesdays from 5pm to 9pm; the **Museum of Anthropology** reduces admission to $10 on Thursday evenings from 5pm to 9pm. For nearly-free walking tours, **Vancouver Tour Guys** (www.tourguys.ca/vancouver) offers four different gratuity-only options (budget for $5 to $10).

LISSANDRA MELO/SHUTTERSTOCK ©

Best Free Attractions

Engine 374 Pavilion The locomotive that pulled the first transcontinental passenger train into Vancouver, preserved in its own Yaletown spot. (p72)

Stanley Park Nature House A fascinating introduction to the flora and fauna of the regional rainforest. (p34)

Kitsilano Showboat Summer-long run of alfresco shows, with the Kitsilano waterfront as a backdrop. (p116)

Morris and Helen Belkin Gallery Free-entry avant-garde art exhibitions at UBC. (p112)

Dr Sun Yat-Sen Classical Chinese Garden & Park A freebie alternative to the paid-entry garden next door, with some of the same classical attributes. (p51)

Survival Guide

Survival Guide

Before You Go

When to Go

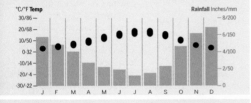

°C/°F Temp
Rainfall Inches/mm

J F M A M J J A S O N D

➡ Winter (Dec–Feb)
Chilly and damp but
perfect for skiing the
local slopes.

➡ Spring (Mar–May)
Rain, some sun and
good hotel rates.

➡ Summer (Jun–Aug)
Vancouver's blue-skied
peak. T-shirts recom-
mended; expect crowded
attractions.

➡ Fall (Sep–Oct) Rain
returns but still some
golden sunny days as the
leaves descend. Another
good time for hotel deals.

Book Your Stay

➡ Vancouver is packed
with visitors every sum-
mer, so book accommoda-
tions far ahead if you're
coming in July and August.

➡ The downtown core and
West End are home to the
greatest concentration
and variety of accommo-
dations options.

➡ Spring and fall shoulder
seasons mean reduced
rates.

Useful Websites

Tourism Vancouver (www.
tourismvancouver.com) Wide
range of accommodations
listings and package deals.

**BC Bed & Breakfast Inn-
keepers Guild** (www.bcs
bestbnbs.com) Wide range
of B&Bs in Vancouver and
around the province.

Lonely Planet (lonely
planet.com/canada/vancouver/
hotels) Recommendations
and bookings.

Arriving in Vancouver

Best Budget

YWCA Hotel (www.ywcahotel.com) Centrally located tower with comfortable rooms that offer great value (especially for families).

Buchan Hotel (www.buchanhotel.com) Close to Stanley Park, its smaller rooms are budget-friendly, especially off-season.

Best Midrange

Skwachays Lodge (www.skwachays.com) New boutique hotel lined with First Nations art.

Sylvia Hotel (www.sylviahotel.com) Charming beachfront sleepover in the West End, overlooking English Bay.

Best Top End

Rosewood Hotel Georgia (www.rosewoodhotels.com) Vancouver's top 'it' hotel for stylish overnighting.

Wedgewood Hotel & Spa (www.wedgewoodhotel.com) Classic deluxe hotel dripping with elegant flourishes.

Vancouver International Airport

➡ Canada's second-busiest airport, **Vancouver International Airport** (YVR; ☎604-207-7077; www.yvr.ca; 🛜) lies 13km south of downtown in the city of Richmond. There are two main terminals – international (including flights to the US) and domestic – just a short indoor stroll apart.

➡ A third (and smaller) South Terminal is a short drive away: free shuttle buses are provided. This terminal services floatplanes, helicopters and smaller aircraft traveling on lower capacity routes to small communities in BC and beyond.

➡ Alongside taxis, limo services and car rentals desks, there is a Canada Line SkyTrain station at the airport that links to downtown.

Pacific Central Station

➡ **Pacific Central Station** (1150 Station St; Ⓢ Main St-Science World) is the city's main terminus for long-distance trains from across Canada on **VIA Rail** (www.viarail.com), and from Seattle, USA (just south of the border) and beyond on **Amtrak** (www.amtrak.com).

➡ Most intercity nontransit buses also arrive at Pacific Central. It's the main arrival point for cross-Canada and trans-border **Greyhound** services (www.greyhound.com; www.greyhound.ca); cross-border budget bus services on **Bolt Bus** (www.boltbus.com); and services from Seattle and Seattle's Sea-Tac International Airport on **Quick Shuttle** (www.quickcoach.com).

➡ The Main St-Science World SkyTrain station is just across the street for connections to downtown and beyond.

➡ There are car-rental desks in the station and cabs are also available just outside the building.

Tsawwassen & Horseshoe Bay Ferry Terminals

➡ **BC Ferries** (☎250-386-3431; www.bcferries.com) services from across the province arrive at Tsawwassen, an hour south of Vancouver, and at Horseshoe Bay, 30 minutes from downtown in West Vancouver.

➡ Main services to Tsawwassen arrive from Vancouver Island's Swartz Bay, near Victoria, and Duke Point, near Nanaimo. Services also arrive from the Southern Gulf Islands.

➡ Services to Horseshoe Bay arrive from Nanaimo's Departure Bay. Services also arrive here from Bowen Island and from Langdale on the Sunshine Coast.

➡ To reach downtown from Tsawwassen on transit, take bus 620 (adult/child $5.50/3.50) to Bridgeport Station and transfer to the Canada Line. It takes about 40 minutes.

➡ From Horseshoe Bay to downtown, take bus 257 (adult/child $4/2.75, 45 minutes), which is faster than bus 250. It takes about 35 minutes.

Getting Around

Bus

➡ Vancouver's **TransLink** (www.translink.ca) bus network is extensive. All vehicles are equipped with bike racks and all are wheelchair accessible. Exact change (or more) is required; buses use fare machines and change is not given. Tickets are valid for up to 90 minutes of transfer travel.

➡ Bus services operate from early morning to after midnight in central areas. There's also a limited night-bus system that runs every 30 minutes between 1:30am and 4am. The last night-bus leaves downtown Vancouver at 3:09am. Look for night-bus signs at designated stops.

SkyTrain

➡ TransLink's SkyTrain network currently consists of three routes and is a great way to move around the region, especially beyond the city center. A fourth route, the Evergreen Line, is planned to link the suburban commu-nities of Burnaby, Coquit-lam and Port Moody.

➡ Tickets for SkyTrain trips can be purchased from station machines.

➡ If you're traveling from the airport on the Canada Line, a $5 airport fee is added to your regular fare at time of purchase.

SeaBus

➡ The iconic SeaBus shuttle is part of the TransLink transit system (regular transit fares apply) and it operates throughout the day, taking 12 minutes to cross Burrard Inlet between Waterfront Station and Lonsdale Quay in North Vancouver. At Lonsdale you can then connect to buses servicing North Vancouver and West Vancouver; this is where you pick up bus 236 to both Capilano Suspension Bridge and Grouse Mountain.

➡ SeaBus services leave from Waterfront Station between 6:16am and 1:22am Monday to Saturday (8:16am to 11:16pm Sunday). Vessels are wheelchair accessible and bike-friendly.

➡ Tickets must be purchased from vending machines on

either side of the route before boarding. The machines take credit and debit cards and also give change up to $20 for cash transactions.

Miniferry

➡ Operators offer day passes ($10 to $15) plus discounted books of tickets for multiple trips. Single trips costs from $3.50.

➡ **Aquabus Ferries** (☎604-689-5858; www.the aquabus.com; adult/child from $3.50/1.75) Runs frequent minivessels (some big enough to carry bikes) between the foot of Hornby St and Granville Island. It also services several additional spots along the False Creek waterfront as far as Science World.

➡ **False Creek Ferries** (☎604-684-7781; www. granvilleislandferries.bc.ca; adult/child from $3.25/2) Operates a similar Granville Island service from Sunset Beach, and has additional ports of call around False Creek.

Taxi

➡ Vancouver currently does not allow Uber-type services. Try the following long-established taxi companies:

Transit Tickets & Passes

➡ Alongside trip-planning resources, TransLink's website (www.translink.bc.ca) explains the fares and passes covering its bus, SeaBus and SkyTrain network.

➡ The network is divided into three zones. One-zone tickets cost adult/child $2.75/1.75, two-zones $4/2.75 and three-zones $5.50/3.75. All bus trips are regarded as one-zone fares.

➡ You can buy single-trip tickets (valid for up to 90 minutes of transfer travel on the entire network), all-access DayPasses ($9.75) or plastic recharge-able Compass Cards ($6 deposit) from SkyTrain and Seabus vending machines. You can only buy single-trip tickets on buses and these are valid for 90 minutes of transfer travel on buses only.

➡ DayPasses and Compass Cards are also sold at Compass retailers around the city, including London Drugs branches.

➡ After 6:30pm, and on weekends or holidays, all transit trips are classed as one-zone fares.

➡ **Black Top & Checker Cabs** (☎604-731-1111)

➡ **Vancouver Taxi** (☎604-871-1111)

➡ **Yellow Cab** (☎604-681-1111)

Bicycle

➡ Vancouver is a relatively good cycling city, with more than 300km of designated routes criss-crossing the region.

➡ Cyclists can take their bikes for free on SkyTrain, SeaBus and transit bus services (all now fitted with bike racks).

➡ Cyclists are required by law to wear helmets here.

➡ Vancouver's recently introduced public bike-share scheme is called **Mobi** (www.mobibikes.ca).

➡ Pick up a free *Metro Vancouver Cycling Map* for details on area routes and bike-friendly contacts and resources – or download it from the TransLink website.

Car & Motorcycle

➡ For most Vancouver sightseeing, you'll be fine without a car; much of the city is easy to explore on foot and via transit.

➡ For visits that incorporate the wider region, a vehicle makes life much simpler: the further you travel from downtown, the more limited your transit options become.

➡ Parking is at a premium in downtown Vancouver: there are some free spots on residential side streets but many require permits, and traffic wardens are predictably predatory. For an interactive map of parking-lot locations, check EasyPark (www.easypark.ca).

Essential Information

Business Hours

Banks 9am–5pm weekdays, with some opening Saturday mornings.

Shops 10am–6pm Monday to Saturday; noon to 5pm Sunday.

Restaurants 11:30am–2pm; 5–10pm.

Coffee shops From 8am, some earlier.

Pubs and bars pubs often from 11:30am; bars often from 5pm. Closing from midnight or beyond.

Discount Cards

Vancouver City Passport ($25; www.citypassports.com) Discounts at attractions, restaurants and activities across the city for up to two adults and two children.

Vanier Park Explore Pass (adult/child $36/30; www.spacecentre.ca/explore-pass) Covers combined entry to the Museum of Vancouver, Vancouver Maritime Museum and HR MacMillan Space Centre. Includes one entry to each attraction and is available at any of the three sites.

UBC Museums & Gardens Pass (adult/child $33/28) Combined entry to all of the University of BC's major attractions. It's valid for several months and also includes additional campus discounts.

Electricity

Type A
120V/60Hz

Type B
120V/60Hz

Emergency

Police, Fire & Ambulance (🖀911)

Police (non-emergency number; 🖀604-717-3321)

Money

Credit Cards

➡ Credit cards are accepted and widely used at all accommodations and almost all shops and restaurants.

➡ Visa, MasterCard and American Express are widely accepted in Canada.

➡ Credit cards can get you cash advances at bank ATMs, usually for an additional surcharge.

➡ Be aware that many US-based credit cards convert foreign charges using unfavorable exchange rates and fees.

ATMs

➡ ATMs are widely available around the city.

➡ Interbank ATM exchange rates usually beat the rates offered for traveler's checks or foreign currency.

➡ Canadian ATM fees are generally low, but your

home bank may charge another fee on top of that.

➡ Some ATM machines also dispense US currency; ideal if you're planning a trip across the border.

Changing Money

➡ You can exchange currency at most main bank branches, which often charge less than the *bureaux de change* dotted around the city.

➡ In addition to the banks, try **Vancouver Bullion & Currency Exchange** (www.vbce.ca; 800 W Pender St; 🕘9am-5pm Mon-Fri; Ⓢ Granville), which offers a wider range of currencies and competitive rates.

Public Holidays

New Year's Day 1 January

Family Day Second Monday in February

Good Friday & Easter Monday Late March to mid-April

Victoria Day Third Monday in May

Canada Day 1 July

BC Day First Monday in August

Labour Day First Monday in September

Thanksgiving Second Monday in October

Remembrance Day 11 November

Christmas Day 25 December

Boxing Day 26 December

Safe Travel

➡ Vancouver is relatively safe for visitors.

➡ Purse-snatching and pickpocketing do occur; be vigilant with your personal possessions.

➡ Theft from unattended cars is not uncommon; never leave valuables visible in cars.

➡ Persistent street begging is an issue for some visitors; just say 'Sorry' and pass on if you're not interested and want to be polite.

➡ A small group of hardcore scam artists also works the downtown core, singling out tourists and asking for 'help to get back home.' Do not let them engage you in conversation.

Telephone

➡ Most Vancouver-area phone numbers have the area code 🖀604, although you can also expect to see ☎778. Dial all 10 digits of a given phone number, including the three-digit area code and seven-digit number, even for local calls. Always dial 1 before other domestic long-distance and toll-free (☎800, 888, 877 etc) numbers.

Cell Phones

➡ Cell phones use the GSM and CDMA systems, depending on your carrier. Check with your cellular service provider before you leave about using your phone in Canada. Calls may be routed internationally, and US travelers should beware roaming surcharges (it can become very expensive for a 'local' call).

Tourist Information

➡ The **Tourism Vancouver Visitor Centre** (Map p32; ☎604-683-2000; www. tourismvancouver.com; 200 Burrard St; ⏰8:30am-5pm; ⑤Waterfront) is a large repository of resources for visitors, with a staff of helpful advisers ready to assist in planning your trip.

➡ Services and info available here include free maps, visitor guides, half-priced theater tickets, accommodation and tour bookings, plus a host of glossy brochures on the city and the wider BC region.

Travelers with Disabilities

➡ Vancouver is an accessible city. On arrival at the airport, vehicle-rental agencies can provide prearranged cars with hand controls. Accessible cabs are also widely available at the airport and throughout the city, on request.

➡ All TransLink SkyTrain, SeaBus and transit bus services are wheelchair accessible. Check the TransLink website (www. translink.ca) for a wide range of information on accessible transport around the region. Head to www.accesstotravel. gc.ca for information and resources on accessible travel across Canada. In addition, download Lonely Planet's free Accessible Travel guide from http://lptravel.to/ AccessibleTravel.

➡ Guide dogs may legally be brought into restaurants, hotels and other businesses in Vancouver. Almost all downtown sidewalks have sloping ramps, and most public buildings and attractions are wheelchair accessible. Check the City of Vancouver's dedicated website (www.vancouver. ca/accessibility) for additional information and resources.

Visas

➡ Not required for visitors from the US, the Commonwealth and most of Western Europe for stays up to 180 days. Required by those from more than 130 other countries.

➡ However, visa-exempt foreign nationals flying to Canada now require an Electronic Travel Authorization (eTA). This excludes US citizens and those who already have a valid Canadian visa.

➡ For more information on the eTA, see www. canada.ca/eta. For visa information, visit the website of the **Canada Border Services Agency** (www.cbsa.gc.ca).

Behind the Scenes

Send Us Your Feedback

We love to hear from travelers – your comments help make our books better. We read every word, and we guarantee that your feedback goes straight to the authors. Visit **lonelyplanet.com/contact** to submit your updates and suggestions.

Note: We may edit, reproduce and incorporate your comments in Lonely Planet products such as guidebooks, websites and digital products, so let us know if you don't want your comments reproduced or your name acknowledged. For a copy of our privacy policy visit lonelyplanet.com/privacy.

John's Thanks

Heartfelt thanks to Maggie for the copious cups of tea supplied during this book's extended write-up phase – and to Max the cat for curling up on my desk without touching the keyboard too often. Thanks also to my brother Michael for generously offering to cover all the bars with me!

Acknowledgements

Cover photograph: Science World, Vancouver, Dan Breckwoldt/Shutterstock©

Contents photograph: Totem poles, Stanley Park, Vancouver, Regien Paassen/Shutterstock©

This Book

This 2nd edition of Lonely Planet's *Pocket Vancouver* guidebook was researched and written by John Lee. The previous edition was also written by John Lee. This guidebook was produced by the following:

Destination Editor
Alexander Howard

Product Editor
Alison Ridgway

Senior Cartographer
Corey Hutchison

Book Designer
Virginia Moreno

Assisting Editors
Imogen Bannister, Janice Bird, Kate Chapman, Carly Hall, Victoria Harrison

Assisting Cartographer
Alison Lyall

Cover Researcher Naomi Parker

Index

Our Writer

John Lee

Originally from the UK, John moved to British Columbia to study at the University of Victoria in the 1990s. Eventually staying and moving to Vancouver, he started a freelance travel-writing career in 1999. Since then, he's been covering the region and beyond for Lonely Planet plus magazines, newspapers and online outlets around the world. Winner of numerous writing awards, he's very active on Twitter and a weekly columnist for Canada's th Globe and Mail national newspaper; catch up with him a www.johnleewriter.com.

Published by Lonely Planet Global Limited
CRN 554153
2nd edition – Jun 2017
ISBN 978 1 78657 698 9
© Lonely Planet 2017   Photographs © as indicated 2017
10 9 8 7 6 5 4 3 2 1
Printed in Malaysia

Although the authors and Lonely Planet have taken all reasonable care in preparing this book, we make no warranty about the accuracy or completeness of its content and, to the maximum extent permitted, disclaim all liability arising from its use.